THIS

1. Seeking the Ox

THIS

Becoming Free

by

MICHAEL GUNGOR
(VISHNU DASS)

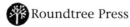 Roundtree Press

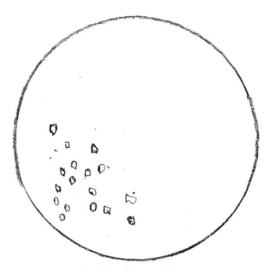

2. Discovering the Tracks

THIS

THIS is all there is.

Yesterday and tomorrow are just wounds and stories.

THIS is not all there is.

There is also *that*—desiring milk while you drink water.

That is suffering.

Of course, *that* is absurd, for *THIS* is all there is.

Does this confuse you, beloved??

Perhaps I could say it a different way?

If I ascend to the heavens, you are there;

If I make my bed in Hell, you are there.

3. Finding the Ox

Intentions

M y editor, Nancy, wisely wondered if addressing the reader as "beloved" in that first little poem might be a little too forward so early in the book. It's a valid concern. The thing is, if someone really good-looking or charismatic were to approach you and tell you with all the right facial expressions, body language, and tone of voice that they love you, your heart would probably melt and you would feel good about it. Others of us have personalities that might lead some to assume that we have played a lot of Dungeons and Dragons. And when people like me, with our unkempt hair and our how-do-you-tie-these-on variety of pants, just come out of the blue and tell you that we love you, it doesn't always come across in the same way as if Oprah or George Clooney or someone whom you know and love were saying it. But just because I like sci-fi, have divergent fashion tastes, and compensate for what some would call a weak chin by sporting a fairly patchy, neck-heavy beard doesn't mean my love for you isn't sincere.

THIS

"But you don't even know me!" says the reader whom I don't know.

Again, this is a valid concern. I might not have a familiarity with the depths of your individual soul. I may not know your name, your specific wounds, what keeps you up at night, or what dreams you have for the future. But those are all just stories. Masks and costumes that, impressive as they may be, don't fool me nearly as much anymore. None of the aspects of your personality, memory, or imagination are the real or fullest You. No, you, the real You, are Life itself, God herself, the All in All that gives rise to stories like *you's* and *me's* and *Clooney's* and *neck beards*. Under it all, there is always and only *THIS*—your very heart and self.

This book, Beloved, is my love letter to you. It's full of stories and ideas and bizarre hippie shit. But it's also full of my heart. Because the real reason I'm writing this is to simply tell you that I love you and to remind you of who you really are under all of those stories of yours.

4. Catching the Ox

THE FIRST NOBLE TRUTH
Life Is Suffering

THE SPA
Part 1 (2012)

The spa where I became an atheist was nice, but you know, Aunt-Rhonda-from-the-suburbs-goes-shopping-at-Ikea nice. Thankfully, it was the middle of the day on a weekday, so there was hardly anybody in there. The young woman at the front desk smiled and greeted me even though she probably wondered what a guy who looked like me was doing in a place like that. My appearance often rides the line between musician and homeless, and this didn't look like the kind of establishment that marketed to either demographic. Normally, I might have made sure to smile extra big and stand up extra tall, holding my shoulders back like my mother always told me to do, trying to assure the young woman that I was gainfully employed and housed and that my credit card would not be declined. Maybe if I'd been feeling better, I would have said something polite about the weather. But not this time. I was in no mood for small talk. *Just get me into that steam room as soon as possible. I've got to get out of my head.*

The nearly constant theological and existential angst spirals had increasingly impeded my social skills as of late. Normal human interactions like a simple and sincere greeting were sullied with an underlying contextual circus in which I desperately tried to make sense of the entire universe through a phrase like "have a good day."

Have a good day? I'm supposed to have a good day while siphoning off the spoils of my privilege, ignoring the tremendous suffering of the world? A good day where I kill another who-knows-how-many living organisms in order to eat and survive? What is a good day in this cruel and cold universe?

Then I would feel guilty.

Come on Michael, you need to show this person love, because God is love, and that love and justice is the arc of the universe, and I am supposed to be the very embodiment of that love in the world.

Then again . . .

Why should I go through the trouble of bending myself toward this supposed subtle arc of divine love in the universe if God doesn't even give enough of a damn to make sure all his little girls and boys in his "good world" have enough food to eat, clean water to drink, or that they don't get sold into the sex trade?

That's the headspace I was in when the young woman at the front desk of the hotel spa greeted me. So, sorry, but I was not in the mood for meaningless pleasantries. I barely said a word. I paid her and made a beeline for the men's locker room.

I wondered what was wrong with me. On paper, life was good. Really good actually. I had parents who loved me. A smart, gorgeous, talented wife and a beloved daughter who was my very heart. I had lifelong, devoted friendships with wonderful people. We owned a comfortable home near the Rocky Mountains with a little backyard that had a fire pit and a sandbox shaped like a pirate ship. Lisa and I had built a successful career together in the Christian music industry. People often stopped us on the street and told us how much our music meant to them. I had everything I needed and nearly everything I'd ever wanted. What was I missing? Why was I so miserable?

I knew. I just didn't want to know.

My whole world was built on a lie.

The spa had really nice showers. Double heads. Incredible water pressure. Man, I loved a good shower. I had a good showerhead at home, but why wasn't it this powerful? Where can one even purchase such a thing? How unfair is the world? Sometimes I wondered why we didn't all just commit suicide and get it over with.

These showers really were exemplary though. I turned both nozzles on as hot as I could handle and stood under the unfairly impressive, nearly scalding jets of water. It was almost enough to make me forget about the whole my-life-is-built-on-a-lie thing. Almost.

It's just hard to enjoy a day at the luxury spa when you're paying for it using fairy tales and violence. I was a sort of pseudo-Christian celebrity living in America. You know . . . the country founded on life, liberty, and the pursuit of happiness and built on the backs of slaves? One nation under God, right? That mythical entity "up there" who watches and judges us and gives us permission to steal land and commit genocide against indigenous people. Everything in my life was built on these skeletons and lies.

I hadn't always been this pessimistic. What made me like this?

Not Okay

"Both speech and silence transgress."
—ZEN SAYING

W hen the Buddha, Siddhārtha Gautama, said "Life is suffering," the world was a different place. Life expectancy was less than thirty years old, as opposed to the current global average of seventy-two. They obviously didn't have air-conditioning, Tylenol, or antibiotics back then. Falling down and scratching your knee could easily become a mortal wound. Getting a cavity could become a living hell on earth with no solutions but the crude instruments and excruciating processes of ancient dentistry. We in "civilized" Western society today have more convenience, comfort, and wealth than anyone in the Buddha's day could have possibly imagined. Still, despite all of the luxuries and conveniences of modern life like accessible food, clean water, cars, chiropractors, therapists, Wi-Fi, and marijuana-infused gummy bears, most of us are still drowning in suffering.

Of course, most readers of this book are probably not currently living in the "Oh God, a bear is eating my arm!" realms of suffering, or else they would likely and wisely be spending their attention elsewhere. Those with the time, resources, education, and ability to sit down and read a book have been afforded a level of privilege that most other people through history have not. Still, let's be honest with ourselves— the Netflix binging isn't working as well as we'd hoped. We're destroying the planet's ability to sustain life. We hate each other. We are afraid. We are ashamed of our bodies and not at home in our own skin. Even if we have the means to avoid the loud versions of suffering like agony or terror, most of us still dwell in duller forms of suffering like depression, anxiety, apathy, or boredom.

Though most of us would much prefer an emotion like boredom over, say, anguish, they both are born of suffering, and both keep us from living a vibrant, full life. It's like eating sand rather than rusty nails. Despite the conveniences that come with a world that has gotten so good at sanitizing death and anesthetizing pain, so many of us still do not live full and satisfied lives. The material suffering of the privileged may be paler and duller than of those whose bodies fuel their luxury, but mental suffering is not bound to class, race, gender, age—a life devoid of color, of love, of joy takes place across the human spectrum. So many of us have central heating and iPhones, but we still can't see the magic of spinning on a blue orb hurtling through space at thousands of miles an hour around a giant burning ball of fusing gases. We live with access to clean water and public education but we fail to notice the absurdity and wonder of all of the space-time and electricity and puffy white clouds and cargo pants and sour bubble gum. We don't hear the music in a bird's song. We don't stop to listen to the wisdom of the old oak tree. We don't feel the gravitas of yet another day of the sun bathing our world with warmth and light. Every day, Earth's atmosphere gifts us with over twenty-three thousand lungfuls of breath, and how many of them do we even pay attention to? Our hearts beat the necessary nutrients for life through our entire body a hundred thousand times a day, but how often do we take all of that work for granted? Most of us are just mindlessly running on autopilot most of the time.

We take a walk down the sidewalk and encounter another sentient Earth being with her own pumping heart and breathing lungs and human brain, which as far as we know is the pinnacle of the complexity and beauty of the universe's evolution to this point, and what do we do? Do we bow in reverence and amazement at this wonder of the universe? Do we gasp in awe as she engages in the millions of subtle, powerful, and unimaginably complex movements—firings of neurons, communication of nerves, constrictions of muscles—necessary for human locomotion? No, we barely notice unless maybe this particular one has huge boobs or unusual pants or is riding a unicycle or something.

This is the human predicament. There is an endless not-okayness at our core.

One

"Distinctions of 'important' and 'unimportant' are surely unknown to the Lord, lest, for want of a pin, the cosmos collapse!"
—PARAMAHANSA YOGANANDA

I have good news for you, friend—the liberation that you seek from a life of suffering and meaninglessness can be found within the period at the end of this sentence. This may sound fantastic and absurd, and of course, it is. But that doesn't mean that it's not true. That period, like every other jot and tittle of this universe, is nothing less than the fullness of an infinite, interconnected, nondual[1] mystery being the ineffable reality that is always and only *THIS*. And to directly experience *THIS* is freedom.

That's a lot of fancy talk for a period. But do you have any idea what went into me typing out the complete first sentence of this chapter and ending it with that insignificant-looking little dot? Do you know how many people had to die for that particular mark to make it onto this page? Do you know how many pig orgasms occurred to get that tiny dot to appear in your conscious awareness? Do you know the eons of evolution and revolution that had to transpire, including all the necessary cultural memetic conditioning that may have made you uncomfortable with the phrase "pig orgasms" being included so early on in a book about spiritual realization? All this and immeasurably more took place in order for that easily overlooked speck to be perceived by your nervous system in tandem with all your previously stored memory of language and grammar and punctuation. That period, dear reader, was 13.77 billion years in the making. Countless wars were fought. Supernovas exploded, asteroids collided, planets cooled and whirled into orbits. Empires rose and crumbled. Suns gave rise to black holes that ended up swallowing up suns. Milk Duds gave rise to soft-bellied guys who ended up swallowing more Milk Duds. Are you understanding what I'm telling you?

---

1. A *negative* (saying what ultimate reality is not) term like "nondual" is often preferred to a positive (saying what ultimate reality is) term like "Oneness" in many spiritual traditions that speak of the interconnectedness of all things. We will explore the usefulness of negative language later in the book.

Dearest reader, how can I explain this? Perhaps we could start by considering how that period was typed on a plastic key on a laptop computer. What amount of evolution and innovation did it take for that key to exist in this precise moment of space-time? How many philosophers, mathematicians, chemists, linguists, physicists, and factory workers were instrumental in the line of necessary work for this laptop computer to have a period key? Try, for a moment, to take in just a fraction of the amount of artistic experimentation, electrical engineering, technological change, business development, and social engineering it took. How many court cases, laws, regulations, contracts, tax codes, dress codes, and fire codes did it take? And that's just for one single key for one single dot that a third-century BCE librarian named Aristophanes thought might be helpful.

How many other moments needed to happen for me to write this particular book with that particular period to this particular you?

For instance, I wrote much of this chapter while riding in an airplane, but I'm writing this sentence on an elliptical machine at a gym.

This one was written in a Chinese restaurant.

This one was written in a combination of places, including riding on an escalator, standing in a perfume shop, sitting in a jury assembly room, and waiting in the surprisingly ornate, marble lobby of a post office.

This book was penned from, and as, a diverse set of happenings, a series of patterns and moments that were all tied together within the stories that I think of as "my life" and "this book." The words were written early in the morning and late at night. It was written in bliss, in tears, in heartache, and in joyous wonder, and with some occasional Duds here and there, but none of these events were cleanly isolated from any of the others. They all bled together in, and as, my life and this book.

And what about you, dear reader? Unless you are the middle-aged Japanese businessman sitting next to me in 12B right now and sneakily glimpsing at my screen, you are reading this book in an entirely different context of space-time than the ones I'm writing these words within. But somehow the incalculable number of events leading to your reading this and my writing it have become strangely intertwined. Not only did you have to experience all of the moments that you have in order to pick up this book and read it but I had to create an imaginary "you" in hopes that the real you would eventually come along and materialize my dream like an observer collapsing a probability wave into a particle. For you to be reading this right "now," the "me" now writing it has to imagine some sort of "you" out there who can, or could someday, read and make sense of these letters and symbols. Who are you in my mind, dear reader? Maybe you're a listener of *The Liturgists Podcast* or my band, Gungor. Perhaps you are a janitor who pulled this book out of the trash at a Southern Baptist seminary. Maybe you are me, proofreading this chapter in a month or two, feeling a little self-conscious about all of the Milk Duds talk and taking stock of your physical fitness by gently poking your belly fat. To summarize this left-of-good-writing-techniques paragraph, regardless of who you really are (the infinite *THIS*), your current experienced "now" is being formed in part by the now of my admittedly inaccurate and illusory imagination of your currently experienced now. Trippy.

It is only with my illusory imagination, of both what sort of person you are and what I would like to say to you, that I'm able to whittle down the vast, interconnected mystery of my present experience into some sort of subjective, finite, manageable, and coherent narrative with which I can construct enough meaning to keep you turning these pages.

For instance, do I want to tell you how, just a minute ago, a flight attendant interrupted my writing to ask me, "Would you like warm nuts?"—which my inner junior high school adolescent found humorous? How and why did I make the decision to write that? A few moments ago, I wasn't planning on writing it. If free will is a thing, I could have chosen to keep that bit of information to myself, but instead I opted for full disclosure. I am doing this for at least two reasons that I can think of. First, I wanted to see if I could weave the moment into the imagined, meaning-making matrix that I'm using to write this book, which happens to depend a bit on chaos and absurdity. Like my grandma used to say, "When life gives you lemonade, there's no need to fuck around with lemons."[2] Secondly, in my illusory imagination of you, you're the type of person who might chuckle or at least be willing to press on beyond the normal and understandable questions about this writer's sanity, out of curiosity about where all of this is headed.

2. She did not ever say this, but I thought my first "f-word" in the book might be more tolerable for people if I blamed it on my grandmother, who was a lovely woman. May she rest in peace.

I admit, this book is off to a bizarre start, but, please friend, bear with me a bit longer before I really bring all of this home because I want to bring aliens into it. "Aliens?" you ask? Yes, aliens with really powerful telescopes that can help you understand that the world you experience is completely subjective.

Imagine that scientifically advanced aliens exist and are looking at the earth through powerful telescopes right "now." What do they see? The answer to that question depends entirely on how far away they are. So imagine that right now, there is an alien named Marge in a star system a million light-years away who's looking through her advanced alien telescope at Earth, watching you read this book. There's no need to be too creeped out at that idea though, because from your perspective, Marge will not see you reading this until a million years from now. That is how long it will take for the light reflecting off of you and this book to make it all the way to her telescope a million light-years away.

Now, let's say that you somehow happen to have gotten your hands on one of these really advanced alien telescopes as well. And let's say that you have also magically acquired the knowledge that Marge is currently watching you and know exactly where she's watching you from. Naturally, you're compelled to turn your own amazing telescope towards the sky and look back at peeping Marge's planet. What do you see? Well, even though Marge is "currently" looking at you from her home planet, what you see when looking back is not Marge, her telescope, or her current planet. What you see through your telescope is Marge's planet a million years ago. She can see you through her telescope, but as you look back, you can't see anything within a million years of her watching you. Weird, right?

Okay, so now let's say that you get frustrated that you can't see Marge even though you know she's there and looking at you and decide to pan your telescope around the night sky a bit to see what else you can find. Luckily, you find another inhabited planet, and alas, you stumble across an alien named Jorge who just so happens to be looking right back at Earth through his own powerful telescope. One might expect to feel startled to look up into the sky and see an alien staring back at you, but not you! Because you have already learned from your experience with Marge, that the telescope views aren't going to be the same. Even though you can see Jorge staring right back at you with his telescope, you know he cannot see you. In fact, in a strange and convenient plot twist, Jorge just happens to be the right distance from Earth to be watching me writing this very chapter.

So to recap, Marge, who is a million light-years away is "currently" (from her perspective) watching you reading this book. You can't see her watching you from your perspective, but you can "currently" see Jorge, who is "currently" watching me write this book, which you will someday read in the future, which means that if he's peeping at my screen like 12B over here, he knows you are watching him before you do. In this scenario, your reading of these words right now is not only happening in your present but also in the future (as seen through Jorge's "now") and the ancient past (as seen through Marge's "now"). How's your brain doing, dear reader?

Here's my point: When you look deeply enough into any one moment, it becomes clear that there is no such thing as an objective or universal "now." This is easier for us to see over long distances like the ones in the above absurd scenario, but the truth and weirdness of special relativity applies even in face-to-face conversation. There is always some sort of lag of the "now" between you and every other observer you ever interact with who is inhabiting a different segment of space-time[3] than you (which is everybody else). Your now is never my now. In fact, a single second of time, up in this airplane that I'm writing in, goes slightly faster than a single second of time down on the ground. Every moment we experience in this universe happens in a completely relative perspective.

As physicist Carlo Rovelli put it, "Our intuitive idea of the present, the ensemble of all events happening 'now' in the universe, is an effect of our blindness: our inability to recognize small temporal intervals."[4] It is that blindness that gives us our sense of reality. It's like how a fire dancer's torch appears as a solid circle of flames as she spins it around her head. It's not actually a circle, but our perception isn't fast enough to keep up with the precise space-time coordinates of the moving light. In short, the reality that you and I are experiencing as you read, and I write, is a lot weirder than it might seem. What you may have thought of as your simple "now" moment of reading this book is really some

---

3. As Einstein showed us in the theory of special relativity, even space and time are not separate from each other.

4. Carlo Rovelli, *Reality Is Not What It Seems: The Journey to Quantum Gravity* (New York: Riverhead Books, 2017).

weird amalgamation or relationship of countless different moments that include dead grandmothers, luxury spas, the US Postal Service, Japanese businessmen, and warm nuts.

That period at the end of the first sentence of this chapter and, for that matter, everything in existence, is happening from and as a long, interconnected web of happenings, all of which are completely interdependent and inseparable from one another. Like an unfathomably complex game of sudoku, every numbered box in this universe belongs exactly as it is within its context. To change one number would be to change them all. You seeing the period in that first sentence is tied to me riding in this airplane, which is tied to my grandfather missing a boat in Turkey and taking a different one, which led him to meeting my grandmother, which is tied to the weather patterns that the boat encountered on its way to America, which is tied to the carbon emissions of the earth, which is tied to how many cows farted in the eighteenth century, which is tied to the size, timing, and precision of every asteroid that ever struck or missed the earth. John Donne wrote that no man is an island. No moment is an island either. All of it goes together.

A common metaphor used in describing the nondual view is that of a wave in the ocean. In order to let that metaphor sink in, consider one more scenario:

Imagine an ocean stretching out before you as far as you can see. The undulating surface of the water extends all the way to the horizon where it merges with the edge of the sky. Waves of turquoise blue crash onto the shore and crawl up to your toes with a slight sizzle of popping sea-foam. Looking out at this endless procession of wave upon wave, you notice one particularly appealing ocean curl rising higher than the rest. This wave is especially intriguing, so you summon the magical powers you didn't know you had and scoop up the wave into a massive, clear glass container to bring back to your home with you. When you arrive, you set the wave container next to your front door—a bold, yet arguably misguided attempt at curb appeal.

As you step back and look at it, you realize something is off. The wave doesn't look at all like it did in the ocean. Before you magically ladled it from the endless stretch of sea into your display case, it was a mighty turquoise cascade crowned with a foamy white crest curling down

into its trough. Now that it's on your doorstep, it looks more like . . .
a large jar of dirty water. This is because waves aren't real and separate
things from an ocean. Waves are the ocean *waving*. Waves are simply
names we use to describe a type of pattern within the movement of the
ocean, but there is no distance or separation between a wave and an
ocean. Waves are oceans doing what oceans do, just as pears are what
pear trees do, and human civilization is what the earth does.

There is nothing in existence that is fundamentally separate from
anything else. The full reality of one particular thing (say, a person) can
never be found by simply adding up the separate constituency of its
parts (heart, lungs, brain, fingernails . . . etc.), but it's in the relationship
between all of those parts and all the other patterns of energy in
its environment (which happens to be everything in the universe).
Thinking of a person as separate from her surroundings that she exists
within (the universe) is as arbitrary as thinking of a flower petal as a
separate thing from a flower. The petal implies a stem, which implies
soil, which implies sunlight, which implies gravity, and so on and so on.
In the same way, a living brain implies a body, which implies organic
matter, which implies a planet a certain distance from a star, which also
implies gravity, and so on. Human feet aren't planted into the ground,
so most of us don't think about how fundamentally connected to the
earth our bodies are, but our roots into the earth are the air we breathe
and the food we eat and the water our bodies are made of. Human
beings may be the wireless upgrade, but they are no less an extension
and substance of the earth than a mountain is. You are literally the
earth. You are the universe doing what the universe does, just as light is
what the sun does or a wave is what the ocean does. You could also see
this in the opposite way—the universe is You doing what You do.

This is not how it feels to most of us because the nerve endings in
our bodies end at our skin. This gives the illusion of some sort of real
boundary between the "inside" and "outside" of our bodies, but if you
look closely enough, there is no such firm line. Our bodies are like a
waterfall—although the specific water molecules in a single waterfall
are never the same from one moment to the next, there is a similar
enough pattern in how the body of water moves (due to our afore-
mentioned blindness to small temporal intervals) for us to think of a

waterfall as a consistent *something*. So we think of a waterfall as a noun rather than a verb. This is exactly how it is with our bodies. The dance between the constantly changing cells, the quantum-leaping electrons, the hundred-trillion neutrinos passing through us at any given moment, the ever-moving kinetic energy of the quarks, or binding energy of the gluons, finds enough of a musical pattern in our particular speed of perception for us to name a *something*. But what you think of as you (or anything else for that matter) is simply movement within the ocean of Being, of *THIS*. Rhythmic pattern within rhythmic pattern. Music within music.

There is literally no end to this string of events that is the universe. You've likely heard of the "butterfly effect"? Well, the truth of the matter is not just that the flutter of a butterfly's wings shapes weather patterns on Earth. The connection between events goes out much farther than that—to cosmological constants and electromagnetic fields and quantum gravity and everything and everyone that has ever been. The shape of your belly button is interdependent with the specific color, density, and shape of a rock on the third moon orbiting planet Z345 in a distant solar system of the Andromeda Galaxy. So, yes, a lot went into the period at the end of that first sentence.

Still, what does any of this have to do with that not-okayness at the core of the human experience? What does seeing the interconnected-ness of everything have to do with the amount of suffering or freedom that I experience? To get there, I'd like to tell you more of my story and why what I experienced in that spa paved the way for an entirely new way of seeing and experiencing the world. I used to feel separate, alone, and afraid. The universe was a big scary place "out there" that I needed to be protected from. I was afraid of death. God was my answer to that fear, but he too was "out there"—an omnipotent being who technically loved me but also watched me, and judged my every thought, attitude, and action. At the end of the day, at the bottom of my stories, I was alone. Hoping to be loved. To be saved. To be okay. But I wasn't okay. For years, I suffered in the darkness of shame, doubt, and repression. I was a prisoner to my circumstances and the stories I experienced them through. I am not a prisoner anymore. I hope that by the end of this book, you will see that you don't have to be either.

It's Not the Soap

T he first time I remember feeling that there was something fundamentally not okay with me was when I was five years old. I was having a playdate at a friend's house (though we didn't call them playdates back then). We were playing house in her bedroom while our parents talked about boring, adult stuff downstairs.

Her name was Daisy. She asked me if I'd like to kiss her. I was afraid, but her asking made my body tingle in a way I had never felt before, and I had the strange and sudden urge to see what she looked like without her clothes on. I'd never seen a girl without her clothes on before and suddenly felt curious.

This was before my world had taught me that my curiosity was evil, before I learned in my Christian school education that physicality and sexuality were part of the "fleshly" world that was not our real home.

So, I asked Daisy if she'd like to take her clothes off. She said that she just wanted to kiss me, but even though I was only five, the genes in my body have had a lot of experience with that sort of thing through their millions of years of evolution, and they were prompting me to make a deal here. I offered Daisy a compromise—I'd be willing to kiss her if she took her clothes off. She agreed to take everything off but her underwear. The parents entered our burgeoning love chamber before anything else happened, and they were not happy with the scene they had discovered.

After we got home, I remember sitting down with my father, feeling so embarrassed, so ashamed of myself. He was my hero. All I wanted was for him to be proud of me. He was the pastor of our church, and Daisy's parents were elders. He didn't need to say it explicitly, but I

27

knew I had embarrassed him. Looking back, I'm sure he wasn't as freaked out as I had thought he was. He probably knew we were just being normal, curious little kids, but at the time, I felt like I had done the worst thing anyone could ever do. I felt that something at the core of me was bad. My mind, my curiosity, my body, they were all evil and could not be trusted.

I resolved to never do that sort of thing again. I wanted to prove to my dad and everyone else out there that I could be better than that. I could be a good and lovable boy. I told my dad that I was so sorry. I buried my head in his chest and wept.

Fast forward a decade and I was the poster boy for evangelical Christianity in my little world in central Wisconsin. I was a straight-A student at my Christian school. I respected my elders, read the One Year Bible every day, and debated the godless evolutionists online. I didn't dare drink, smoke, or cuss. I wore a purity ring that my dad gave me as a sign of my vow to not have sex until I was married.

Here is a word-for-word segment of a journal entry from when I was sixteen:

> Lord God of Heaven, Creator of the universe, omnipotent, awesome Lord, I worship you. Help me God as I start to have my qt's [quiet times] again. Touch me. Give me the grace I need. I need a lot. Give me your grace for the remainder of this day, Lord. Teach me your wonderful ways, Lord. I will not walk in sin and condemnation. I will not listen to the lies of the evil one. I will worship. I will magnify and exalt the Lord my God and offer my life as a sacrifice, holy and pleasing to Him. Make me like your tool made of gold, Lord. I give you all the glory. To you be the majesty, glory, power, dominion, lordship, honor and praise. Thank you, God. Holy Spirit, help me, be my help. I trust you. In Jesus' mighty Name, Amen. Woo! Oh yeah, we went witnessing last week, and I got to minister to Ana. Bless her Lord. Convict her, touch her, reveal yourself.

As you can see, I was all in. While other kids were out partying and having sex, I was at home journaling about "Lordship." On weekends, I'd sometimes get together with my friends and have worship nights in our living rooms. I was a musician, but I only wrote songs to God. I didn't even listen to secular music because I didn't want to pollute my spirit.

I didn't date anyone until I was a senior in high school. She was a fellow preacher's kid and a fellow worship leader. We used to sing Hillsong worship duets together, and that was sort of like our version of first base. We dated (or *courted*, thank you very much) for six months, but we never kissed. (I wasn't about to relive the Daisy fiasco!) I didn't even say the word *butt* when I was with her because I wanted to be a godly young gentleman. It was not a *butt*. It was a *rear end*, thank you very much. #lordship.

I did go out on a limb and kiss her hand once, but we were warned by her parents that we were moving too fast. (You know how it goes. Step one: worship duets. Step two: hand kissing. Step three: anal beads.)

She and I were voted homecoming king and queen because of our laudable display of godliness, and I won the coveted "King David" award at my Christian high school. I spent many of my lunch breaks fasting and praying and trying to overcome any hand-kissing or masturbatory inclinations or desires. (I was a good boy, right Dad?)

I needed to be good. I needed God to fix me so I could be okay.

I'd like to offer you some context now for that lordship journal entry that I shared with you earlier. That particular journal entry was folded and then thoroughly taped shut, with a note on the folded page that said DO NOT READ. After prying it open, the intruder would then find at the top of the page, a second line of defense. I had scrawled in desperate red letters:

> WHOEVER IS READING THIS PLEASE! STOP! THIS IS VERY
> PERSONAL. PLEASE!⁵

The beginning of the journal reads as follows:

> Today, I led worship in chapel and nobody entered in. Am I losing the
> anointing for this mast [note: the word "mast" was scrawled very
> sloppily to be intentionally illegible because it meant masturbation]
> thing? I just did it again a second ago. I hate this life SO much. I keep
> sinning every day so much and I don't seem to care because I'm faithful

---

5. I feel like I should offer my apologies to my teenage self who hoped those desperate pleas would accomplish something. He would not have been thrilled to hear that his future self would share that journal entry with the world in a book. Oh well.

to do it the next day. The problem is, I know all the right stuff. I know to memorize and quote scriptures. For instance—Jude 24, 1 Cor 10:13, 2 Cor 5:17, Romans 12:1-2 . . . etc. I know them, but when temptation comes, I don't quote them. I know to cry out for help to God, but if I do, it will pass for a second and then come back later. I always give in. I figure if I've already started I might as well finish. I can just repent later. How pathetic! Why am I doing this to myself? Why do I give into Satan and despise God in sin? Why do I willingly give up my anointing for a brief second of painful pleasure? Painful because I know I'm sinning. I may have even violated our covenant today [note: I must have had some "covenant" with God not to look at something]. Michael . . . Why? . . . Jesus. Jesus. Father, what do I even say . . .

Jesus was my answer to that gnawing sense of brokenness at the center of my being. I was told Jesus could heal me. He could make me clean and take away my shame. By following him and being pure, I could live in the light and vanquish the shadows that haunted me. I just needed more passion, more faith, more humility in order to be who I was supposed to be! But the more passionate I became about becoming pure, the more shame I felt for not fully living up to my purity ideals. This created a strange sort of cycle in my life—a self-reinforcing loop where more shame led to more passion which led to more shame.

Of course, all of this religious zeal did have its perks. I got my first megachurch worship leader job in high school. By the time I was twenty, I was leading a music department of over a hundred people. I was married to my second and final girlfriend, Lisa. She wasn't quite as puritanical as the first girl, and my purity ring ended up a bit dented both literally and metaphorically, but we technically made it to the purity culture finish line. We built a house. I had a small staff that answered to me. I had a company car, and my schooling was paid for. By the time I was thirty, I was a Grammy-nominated, Dove Award–winning Christian musician traveling the world, leading worship in churches, clubs, theaters, arenas, and even a few stadiums. We had moved to Denver and started a church in our living room called "Bloom." It was small, but it was young and vibrant and full of beautifully unrealistic dreams about changing the world.

Through all of these years of following Jesus, I had witnessed a pretty broad swath of Christendom. I had been on the stages of the largest churches in the country and the living rooms of some of the smallest. We had played, visited, and worshipped with nearly every Christian denomination I'd ever heard of. We had played Christian festivals, universities, and the conferences of the largest evangelical Christian movements like Hillsong, Passion, Catalyst, Willow Creek, Saddleback, Acquire the Fire, National Worship Leader Conference, and the like.

In other words, I had succeeded. I got what I wanted—to live my life in worship of God with the people of God. To play a significant role in the work of the Lord on the earth. I always thought that all of this would have made me okay. But I still wasn't okay. In fact, it was almost as though as all my dreams came true, I was becoming more and more miserable. I was like a kid who had stayed up all night next to the Christmas tree waiting to open his presents only to discover in the morning, one by one, that every box was filled with broken glass. The accolades hadn't made me love myself. The applause hadn't provided the ground for my being that I had hoped it would. I felt alone, confused, and angry. I had thought a life dedicated to the faith would lead me to a place of peace and love, but through all of the years of experiencing the backstage underbelly of evangelical Christendom, I had slowly and steadily become less and less certain that the faith of my childhood was good, let alone true.

I began to question the validity of the idea of a loving God. In my mission trips and other travels, I had seen some of the harshness and extreme poverty in places like Mexico, Costa Rica, Brazil, Jamaica, China, Thailand, the Philippines, Siberia, Uganda, South Africa, and Kenya, and I knew that I hadn't even seen the worst of it. I once visited Auschwitz—the piles of children's shoes and mounds of hair had forever annihilated any remaining simplistic concepts I had about God's goodness or providence.

When I looked at all the war, abuse, racism, sexism, bigotry, greed, inequality, poverty, sickness, fear, and suffering of the world and contrasted it to what I believed about the God who was supposedly sovereign over the world, it just didn't add up for me.

Omnipotent + All good + Omniscient + Sovereign = the Holocaust?

Nope. That didn't work. Over the years, I had tried tinkering with each of those variables in the equation. I had tried tweaking the "omnipotent" variable with a free will/Fall caveat, à la C. S. Lewis and friends who argued that true love demanded freedom. If we weren't free to choose to love God or not love God, how could it really be love? We as a species had chosen to not love, and it was this "original sin" of humankind that was responsible for all the evil in the world. But I ultimately found the attempt, valiant as it was, to explain away billions of years of death and entropy by blaming it on human sin a bit far-fetched and narcissistic.

I had flirted with the ideas of Calvinism for a while. Calvinism had solved the problem of evil by arguing that God was sovereign over it and was glorified in everything, even in things like the Holocaust that we humans couldn't understand. In debating through some of the ideas with a Calvinist friend about how a good God could be ultimately responsible for sending people to be tormented in a lake of fire for eternity, it was explained to me that diamonds are often displayed at jewelry stores not on gold or other shiny surfaces, but on black velvet. The idea of God not only being responsible for the evil of the world but doing it because it somehow made him look better in comparison to his horrible creation was not an acceptable solution to the problem. In fact, it seemed to me that trying to solve the problem of evil by making God responsible for that evil was a bit like trying to solve the problem of not being able to come to a consensus on where to eat with your friends by slaughtering and eating your friends. I had no interest in worshipping or believing in any sort of god who created glory for himself by burning his children alive for all eternity. I'd much prefer Deism (the belief that God created the universe but doesn't interact with it) or even atheism to that. A cold, meaningless, godless universe would be a far better reality than one in which most of the beings within it wind up spending their eternity in conscious torture.

I became an open theist for a while. Open theism solves the conundrum of God's goodness in the midst of evil by tweaking the "omniscient" variable, positing that God's omniscience would not necessarily extend to a future which does not yet exist. This is basically another theological loophole for free will, but ultimately left me unconvinced given the fact that space-time doesn't behave in a linear and humancentric way. The theory of relativity reveals that our human experience of time (a series of separate events) is completely relative to our speed and location through space. Like my friend, Science Mike, once eloquently stated when we were both a little drunk, "Human beings exist somewhere in the middle of a photon and a singularity."[6] If a photon could see, it would see past, present, and future as one single "event." Wouldn't an all-powerful God transcend space-time at least as much as a photon?

By the time I would lose God at the luxury spa in 2012, my religious views had zigzagged across the theological spectrum of Christendom as I searched for the truth that could set me free, that could solve that fundamental sense of not-okayness at the center of my being. This would all turn out to be an exercise in futility.

Most parents are wise enough to know that if their exhausted toddler throws a tantrum when a soap commercial interrupts her YouTube videos, the most effective solution would probably not be to write an email to YouTube, demanding that they ban all soap or soap-related commercials from their platform, or to start a neighborhood petition to boycott all soap until all their children's YouTube-related tantrums have disappeared. The problem isn't the soap.

I, on the other hand, was not so wise, as I spent decades of my life trying to chase away the shame and malaise at my core by adjusting the dials on my theological assumptions monitor. I thought that I could be fixed if I could just think the right thoughts, understand the right concepts, live a pure-enough life. *Then* I could be okay.

But the problem was never the soap.

---

6. A singularity in physics is an infinitely small, one-dimensional point that could contain all of the mass and space-time in the universe in which all of the laws of physics break down.

Broken (1999)

S omething was off. Why hadn't my dad shown up to service? He always showed up, especially to Friday-night service. He was the pastor of a hip and quickly growing megachurch.

We had gone from zero to three thousand people in just a few years, and our Friday-night service was one of the hottest events in south Tulsa. He almost never missed it. None of us did.

As the mob of people, most of whom were college students, flooded in from the line of traffic on Garnett Avenue, they were met with the smiling faces, and often-costumed bodies of the parking ministry golf cart drivers. The congregants were dropped off at the front door where the balloons, candy, and high-energy music welcomed them to a church service like they had never experienced before.

I was the worship leader, and our worship team was the Dave Matthews Band of the Oklahoma church music scene. With lightning-fast acoustic guitar licks, heart-pounding djembes, and soul-rending soprano sax solos, Friday-night worship was like making love with my apparently very skilled next-door neighbor in college—sweaty and loud and it lasted at least an hour. Sometimes it went so well, my dad would decide to spontaneously keep the music going the whole service. Those nights were always especially exhilarating. People would sometimes yell out songs they wanted to sing. There would be extended improvisation and singing "in the Spirit," which usually sounded like people singing between the dominant and tonic notes of the scale with phrases like, "We ascribe greatness unto thee," or "Deeba Rojo Seta Keeno" for the most charismatically adventurous among us. My dad's singing in the Spirit was always a little more sophisticated than the average person's and always tended to sound a bit Caribbean somehow. (He is Puerto

Rican, but he grew up in Neillsville, Wisconsin, so I'm not quite sure where his musical influences came from.)

As one of the hordes of horny Christian college boys there seeking wives, I can attest that the Friday-night scene wasn't made any worse by all the sexy college girls lifting their arms to the sky and writhing in spiritual ecstasy. This particular Friday night was one of those that had spontaneously turned into an all-music night, but this time it wasn't because my dad had given me the nod to keep going. He simply hadn't shown up. I was worried and immediately talked to one of the associate pastors after service to see what had happened. I was told to head straight home.

I tried calling. No answer. I rushed home.

When I arrived, my mother was a wreck. Why hadn't she answered? What had happened? Was he hurt? Worse?

"He left us," she whimpered. She handed me his cell phone. He had left it, too.

"What do you mean he left us?"

She told me that he had an extended affair with a close family friend. And now he was gone. He left us for her.

The world turned red. I smashed the phone against the wall.

My problem was never really about my beliefs. It went much deeper than that.

Shoes on the White Couch

T his was not who our family was supposed to be. We were not supposed to be just another religious leader's sex-scandal story. We were better than that. My father was better than that. He had been my mentor. My hero. He always said how, aside from God, our mother was the most important part of his life and his primary spiritual responsibility was loving her well. He wrote a book called *Supernatural Relationships*.[7] He had taught me that you don't even look at naked girls that you aren't married to, let alone have sex with them.

I once watched him tearfully preach about how cheating on my mom would be the last thing he'd ever do because of the consequences it would have. He talked about how he'd have to face God, and himself. He'd have to face them, his congregation, and how painful that would be. He'd have to face my mom and see her heart broken. And worst of all, he'd have to face his kids and tell them how he had betrayed them and their mom. Maybe that was why he left.

As the thoughts and questions began to pile up in my mind, I did the only thing I knew to do—I picked up my guitar and began to sing worship songs. Crisis has the tendency to reveal the deep parts of our hearts, beliefs, and identities. And the deepest parts of my heart, belief, and identity were all aligned with the idea of me being a worshipper. King David (whose Victory Christian School award, you may recall, I was the esteemed recipient of) was a sinner who did horrible things like murder and adultery, but he apparently worshipped God a lot, and I was told that it was because of that he was called "a man after God's own heart." That's the kind of man I aspired to be. That's how I believed I could eventually be okay.

7. Ed Gungor, *Supernatural Relationships: How to Get Closer to the People You Care For* (Ministry Research Foundation, 1992).

So, on that mournful Saturday, as I thought of the story where David's playing drove the evil spirit and torment out of King Saul, I did the only thing I knew to do. We sat in the living room on the nice white couch together and sang old church songs like "You Are My Hiding Place" and "Great Is Thy Faithfulness." I hoped the words were true. Normally, my mom didn't want us sitting on the nice white couch in the living room. That couch was for looks and could possibly be of use when we had special guests at the house, but otherwise, the rule was stay off. And if you had your shoes on while sitting on it, you were basically taking your life into your own hands. But today she didn't care about the white couch or even whether any of us were wearing shoes. Today, we just sat together, emotionally devastated, but together at least. Most of us anyway.

We'd cry. We'd sing. And cry some more. And then someone somehow got a hold of him on the phone and the room erupted into a frenzy. My nine-year-old sister got on the phone and cried and begged for Daddy to come home. I eventually snatched the phone from her and asked my answerless father who he planned on taking care of his kids for him. Who would be a father for David, who was just a kid still? Who would walk Lissa, his little girl, down the aisle when she got married? We begged him. We told him that we would forgive him, and he should just come home. Come home now. We love you. Please. Come home.

I was furious, of course. More than furious; I hated him for what he had done. His life seemed to me to be the worst kind of lie, but I could not let myself feel that. I had to do what needed to be done for him to come home. I had to step up and be a strong man of God for my family.

· · · · ·

I sat on the floor in my parents' bedroom with my guitar and my new fiancée, Lisa. Lisa and I once again sang "You Are My Hiding Place" in harmony, tears rolling down our cheeks. Lying in the bed, sobbing, were both of my parents. My dad had come home. He had told us he was so sorry. He was a coward. He was a liar. He wanted to make it right. I hated him. But of course, I still loved him. He was my dad. I'd always love him. His face was under the pillow. My mom held his hand, but she didn't look too happy about it.

We sang "Great Is Thy Faithfulness" with thick, stifled voices between the sobs. This time, I believed the words were true.

Bitter

I remained seated in the pew Friday night while everyone around me rose up. They had all erupted into a standing ovation for the associate pastor who had taken over the church with *such wisdom and grace, hadn't he?!* No, he had not. These people were clueless. They had no idea what had been going on behind the scenes.

A few days earlier, this emotionally unstable pastor had scolded me sternly for being manipulated by my parents because I had dared to question his decisions. His decisions had included posting armed guards at the church to make sure my dad didn't come back. *Armed guards.* My dad had no interest in coming back, but this pastor needed to make his new authority and power known. Neither my mom nor dad were allowed anywhere near the church ever again. Never allowed to apologize. Never allowed to grieve or heal within the community they had started. The church's decisions had not only robbed my parents of their much-needed community but of his retirement as well. I was still really pissed at my dad, so I had a little extra patience with this pastor's harsh treatment of him. But my mom? Why punish the victim?

At home I told my dad he had no room to whine about anything. He did this to himself. He accused me of being manipulated by the associate pastor at work. Why was I taking the church's side? Didn't I see how cruel they were being to him and my mother?

I am a 5 on the Enneagram. That means that I have often tried to find my security and worth with information and knowledge. When I experienced the relational firestorm unleashed throughout my life as a result of my dad's affair, I didn't want to admit that I was being anything but objective in my judgments. I was not biased. I saw things how they really were. And everybody but me was batshit crazy.

I couldn't understand why people couldn't just see the truth. It was simple. Right was right and wrong was wrong. I was disgusted by the emotional groupthink that I saw all around me, and I was completely blind to where it existed in me. I didn't see then, or through the next decade and a half of suffering while trying to make the world make sense, how intrinsically my "pure" ideas—what was right or wrong, true or untrue—were tied to my tribe. I couldn't see how my view of Heavenly Father would be filtered through and largely determined by my experience of earthly father. I couldn't see how my experience of my local church formed my view of the universe. I couldn't see how deeply and inextricably my "rational" thoughts were tied to my emotional wounds.

So when part of my tribe stood to mindlessly slap their phalanged meat hooves together for the man who was tearing my sense of tribal belonging apart, I was angry. I thought my anger was about *truth, reason,* and *righteousness*. This was not about my feelings being hurt or that I felt lonely and alienated—I was stronger than that! It was that I was too smart to condone this sort of facade. Everything was not alright, and I would not bow down or play nice within this kind of foolish and misguided Christianity—this oppressive power system that uses shame and manipulation to maintain power. No. *Screw all of this.* While they all stood and applauded him for a difficult job well done, I sat. I sat with all of the sit I could muster. I wore a hard scowl across my face and a visceral clench in my chest.

Church Boy

L isa and I had left Tulsa shortly after we got married in 2000. Things had gotten so stressful at the church, and it had spilled into our entire lives. We could hardly go out on a date without being interrupted by somebody coming up to our table and asking what was going on with the church or my parents. So when a big church in west Michigan offered me a job as their worship leader, I said yes. I went from leading barefoot, sweaty, sexy college-kid megachurch worship to west Michigan, Dutch-reformed-turned-mildly-charismatic, Banana Republic suit–wearing, seventeen-minute megachurch worship.

I was twenty. My assistant was my mother's age. I had a staff and a choir and a company vehicle. One Easter Sunday, Pastor Duane showed a graphic of Earth that showed its geological layers: crust, mantle, core, and hell. Duane may not have been a sophisticated theologian or a geologist, but he and his wife, Jeannie, were authentically kind people. Duane was a good ol' country boy. He was from Michigan, but he somehow spoke with a southern accent. It was once reported to me that his schedule was exactly the same every day. Reportedly, he gets up every morning at 5 A.M., shoots his bow and arrow for an hour, comes back inside to have sex with Jeannie, runs ten miles and is at work by 8 A.M. sharp. Even if that's not entirely accurate, it is absolutely accurate. That's just Pastor Duane. Pastor Duane would go to fine steak restaurants and make them bring him a full bottle of Heinz ketchup from the back, and he'd use most or all of that bottle. One time, a Heinz salesman saw how much ketchup he was eating and bought his meal for him. As a lover of ketchup, I must say that I respect the hell out of Duane for that.

I had spoken to Duane occasionally of how the church in Tulsa had treated my parents after my dad's affair. He responded by showing more grace to my parents than any other pastor on planet Earth. Eventually, he even invited my dad to speak at the church in Michigan. My parents had been in counseling, and it had been a couple years since the affair, and Duane said that he would love to be the first to extend such an offer to them. My parents were moved with gratitude beyond words by the kindness that church showed them. This meant a lot to Lisa and me as well. We had seen my dad leveled. He had become a shell of the man he once was. As much as I or anyone else had hated him in the aftermath of the affair, he had hated himself more. I had forgiven him and wanted him to heal. We ended up staying at that church for several years, largely because of the kindness there. But in the long run, the theology and dress code of the Michigan Dutch were a bit too restrictive for the free, hippie spirits of my wife and me.

We had also grown weary of the whole megachurch scene. As a young married couple with a burgeoning music brand, we had sort of become celebrities at the church. We would spend a lot of Sunday afternoons signing autographs outside the church coffee shop. We grew tired of this, and eventually we left Michigan to tour our music and start a church in Colorado where we could practice our faith more authentically. (Translation: Maybe I could finally become the kind of person I thought I was *supposed* to be, and finally be okay.)

Then came Bloom. Our dream. Our baby. Duane had offered to send us off with some money to start the church if we could wait a little while, but we didn't feel right about that. We didn't want to have any strings attached to anybody. By this point, we had largely given up hope for any sort of organized religious expression, but Bloom was our last-ditch effort to see if there was a way to organize without becoming corrupt. We didn't want there to be anybody but ourselves to blame for any hypocrisy, so we kept it clean and simple. We met in homes at first, and then upstairs at an old community center. Only a few people would come. It was basically a handful of twenty-somethings and a beautiful, old man named Chuck with a wizard-like gray mustache that eventually grew its way all the way down to his nipples. Bloom was a weird place. There was a kid named Cody who played the piano while his pet rat rested on his shoulder. There was a well-endowed homeless girl who kept her cell phone in her cleavage and was more than happy to take her calls in the middle of service. It was fantastic.

We didn't really have official church things like "staff" or "membership." Everyone was welcome and part of us if they wanted to be. We gave away any money in the offerings that was left after paying the rent for the theater. We would do things like go downtown and hand out watermelon slices at the gay pride parade while wearing T-shirts that said, "God loves everyone." Lisa and I would fly in on our own dime every Sunday from wherever our band was touring because we loved Bloom. We also needed it.

The road can be a rough place for a Christian musician. Churches, conferences, festivals, and radio appearances . . . all of which use the name of Jesus to justify their own existence, and most of them exist in the world in a way that has very little to do with the teachings of Jesus. Jesus is so often used as a marketing ploy for the advancement of power-hungry men. And for someone who genuinely loves Jesus, this can be off-putting to say the least. Bloom was our shelter. Our sanctuary. Our home. But it wasn't enough. The Christian world we had seen made me wonder if our religion was true. Were these corrupt, selfish, manipulative people really the one, true, chosen people of God simply because they believed some bizarre and magical claims about a guy rising from the dead? Also, if this was true, wouldn't the people who were supposed to be the "Body of Christ" have more in common with the teachings of the Christ than this? This was a disturbing thought because it jeopardized not only my beliefs, but my very identity and sense of worth.

The Altar (2009)

I knelt at the altar in the front of the dimly lit chapel. No one else was in there. Not even God.

"Where are you?" I asked. "Please . . ."

My words fell from my lips into an infinite, uncaring abyss of nothingness. There was no one to hear them. No one to care.

"Please, Jesus . . . I need your help. I don't have the strength to keep believing. I need you."

The abandoned chapel was in a basement of a church where our band was playing. I had seen too many churches like this one. Churches with American flags on their stages. Pastors who treated their ministries like egoic phalluses. Behind the scenes, they would show me ornate swords in their offices or pictures of majestic animals they had slaughtered on their hunting trips to Africa. Why were all these pastors men? And what was it about testosterone that makes so many men feel like their only life options are kill, fuck, or pastor?

I was so tired of religious hypocrisy. I was tired of the sexism, racism, and religiously powered bigotry. I was so tired of the pointless and embarrassing game of chasing Christian celebrity. Sure, we had Bloom, but after a couple years of such fervent idealism, I had begun to grow weary. We had hoped that our love would change the world, but it hadn't. The church was small and poor and all of our effort felt like a drop of futility in an ocean of pain. The Christianity we had dreamed about seemed to be nothing but that—a dream.

As I knelt in the lonely, silent chapel that night, I watched my faith slipping away from me, and it was terrifying. To lose God would have been worse than losing my life. God was the reason for my life. My faith in and love of God was the only reason I had any worth as a human being. I could *not* lose that.

WALKING MY DOG IN THE RAIN

A Parable (Part 1)

Hi, my name is Fred, and I've been trying desperately not to walk my dog in the rain. What kind of lunatic, after all, would walk his dog while it's raining? Not me, that's for sure! I mean, I'm not perfect. I mess up from time to time—I am only human, but I really have been trying hard. Some people are confused by my constant vigilance against such a filthy and irresponsible behavior as walking my dog in the rain.

"Lighten up, Fred!" they say, when they see me beginning to panic as the storm clouds roll in. "It's just rain."

"Fred, why are you pacing? What are you muttering about?" they ask.

Well, I'll tell you what I'm muttering about! I'm praying that God will help me to not walk my dog in the rain! "God, help me this time," I'll say. "I promise you I'm not going to do it this time. As much as I may want to, I know the consequences just aren't worth it. Who, after all, wants to smell a wet dog or a person who smells like a wet dog? Also, what about my clothes? My shoes? They could be ruined! No, walking dogs in the rain is not good. It's financially and socially irresponsible, and I know that it's against my truest nature. Please, God, give me the grace to not walk my dog in the rain again today."

I've had several long streaks of not walking my dog in the rain in the past, but lately I've had a harder time making my successes stick. Every time I see that the weather forecast includes a high chance of precipitation, I get that familiar pit in my stomach. I know it's coming. I know myself.

At some point, I will panic. I'll go outside with my dog and watch the dark rain clouds roll in, praying and hoping that it's all just a mirage or that maybe this time the clouds will pass overhead and spare us yet another potential humiliation.

Occasionally they do. Occasionally my dog and I wait long enough for a blue sky to appear again, and then we can either go back inside or go for a stroll with that sense of pride and accomplishment. And I'll think to myself, "Perhaps, by the grace of God, I *can* finally stop walking my dog in the rain once and for all."

45

Meaningless

I t's white people.

Well, and patriarchy.

Oh, and capitalism.

And, of course, those racist Republicans.

Or you're looking at it from a different story—it's those gosh-darn, bleeding heart, snowflake liberals who want to take away our guns, take away our freedom of speech, and kill all the unborn babies. All the godless coastal elites constantly pumping their Hollywood propaganda, scientific mumbo jumbo, and pornography into the minds of our young!

It's religion.

Or maybe it's the Devil.

Or maybe it's people who walk their dogs in the rain.

Whatever it is, it's what's wrong with this world. It's these damned young people and their lack of respect for authority. Or it's the old farts who just need to die and free up some seats on the bench. It's *if I only*:

had a better job . . .

had a boyfriend . . .

had more money . . .

lost some weight . . .

could just quit smoking . . .

were more spiritual . . .

Then I'd be okay.

But is that true?

Think about it—if all of your candidates of choice were elected, and they passed all of the bills you wanted them to, do you really think all of humanity would just be entirely okay at that point? Even if every person on Earth finally got access to clean water, education, housing, and a basic income, if all militaries were scrapped and everyone became vegan and there was no more war, famine, racism, or homophobia, would suffering cease to exist? Or from the other side of the culture wars—if everybody on Earth said the sinner's prayer, read their Bible every day, got a job and a haircut and stopped all that goddamned kneeling when people sing the national anthem, would humans finally and completely be at peace in their souls? Of course not. We would find something else to fight about, a different scapegoat to crucify, another group to feel superior to.

Even if you got that dream job and the perfect body and the life partner and the best friend and that harem of porn stars to feed you grapes and fulfill your every whim and desire, you could still find a reason to suffer. You could still be afraid of losing it all. Or you'd start getting suspicious that your friends just loved you for your money. Or all the public attention would make you feel like you were losing yourself. Or maybe you would just find all of the wealth, power, and pleasure empty.

> "Meaningless! Meaningless!"
>   says the Teacher.
> "Utterly meaningless!
>   Everything is meaningless."[8]

The truth is that most of us are playing a game that can't be won. We are hamsters thinking that we can break out of this cage if we just run fast enough on this wheel.

This is the futility of desiring *that* rather than loving *THIS*.

And *that*, as Buddha's second Noble Truth reveals, is the root of all suffering.

5. Taming the Ox

THE SECOND NOBLE TRUTH

Suffering Is the Attachment to Desire

Suffering

———————

"The raindrops patter on the basho leaf, but these are not tears of grief; this is only the anguish of him who is listening to them."
—ZEN SAYING

Here are two short stories to help elucidate this second Noble Truth.

SHORT SUFFERING STORY 1

Whether it's steam rooms, hot tubs, hot springs, or just a good old-fashioned long, hot shower, I'm usually a fan of anything that involves hot water and minimal clothing, but one of my all-time favorite ways of nudely submerging into a soup of kinetically active dihydrogen monoxide is by floating in sensory deprivation tanks. If you don't know what that is, it is a completely dark and silent tank filled with body temperature salt water that allows your relaxed, supine body to simply float within. Normally our brains are taking in an incredible amount of sensory information from the world around us that we aren't even consciously aware of—the hum of the air conditioner, the color of that lady's purse, all the beeps, coughs, and scents of the office, etc. When you get into an environment like a float tank and shut all of that sensation and noise off, it's amazing what your mind will do with all of that freed-up RAM. It's like meditation on steroids. So yes, I'm a regular member at my local float establishment.

As a spiritual explorer, I once tried creating a sort of *mega-float* in order to, you know . . . see what would happen. I booked a two-and-a-half-hour time slot. I had done several of those long sessions before and had always come out feeling pretty trippy. I tended to lose any sense of ego separateness pretty drastically in there, and after that long, I would usually come out sort of forgetting that I'm supposed to be a "someone." Well, this particular time, I thought it would be interesting to try to "enhance" the long floating experience with some natural California "medicine." While I do prefer sobriety as my go-to state of consciousness, I have found the occasional jaunt into other ways of experiencing reality to be enjoyable and even helpful. But this. . . . The hundred-and-fifty-minute float combined with the enhancements was a bit too much. I wouldn't recommend it. (And they don't either. Sorry, float place.) My normal ego loss of a long float was so extreme that in leaving, I walked face-first right into a glass wall.

Strangely, there wasn't enough of an ego in the experience to feel any desire or aversion, and therefore there was no suffering. There was pain. Or perhaps it would be more accurate to say that there was a lot of sensation. It was like an explosion of sensation happened, but it didn't happen to "me," as there was no me for it to happen to. I just remember looking at the sensation of what I wondered might be a broken nose, fascinated with how vivid the sensation was. But absolutely zero suffering.

SHORT SUFFERING STORY 2

My doctor had spotted a small bit of blood in a urine sample and told me that they would have to get in there and take a look to make sure it wasn't cancer or anything. I nodded my head, wondering how exactly they planned on doing that.

"So we should just go ahead and do that now," he said.

"Okay." He still had not explained how this would be done. I understood human anatomy well enough to know that there is a passageway from the external world to the bladder, but I really did not want anything going in there. That's a strict one-way road down there for me. I felt foolish for having to ask for clarification, but I really needed to know what I was in for.

"So, is this like an X-ray thing or . . . ?" I asked, holding out hope.

"No, we'll have to put a scope up there to see in your bladder."

My stomach dropped.

"Put a scope . . ."

"Into your penis, yes."

"Oh, I see. Well, you really think we need to do this today . . . ?"

"Yeah, we need to make sure everything is okay down there. Let's get you over to the nurse so she can wash you up."

And so she did. And as she did, I tried to breathe and calm myself down. Maybe this wouldn't be so bad. I mean, with what our technology is these days, it would probably be like a fishing line or something that I wouldn't even be able to feel. I still didn't like the idea of something going up that way, but it probably was going to be fine. Then the doctor brought in the device that would be inserted into my urethra, and I nearly passed out just looking at the size of that thing. To my eyes, it might as well have been a freaking garden hose. That thing was *thick*, and the camera on the top was *THICKER!* It looked like it was probably state-of-the-art technology in 1976.

"I've got a small camcorder at the house, Doc, maybe we should just use that? It would be a little smaller," I wish I would have said. Instead, the blood drained from my face and yes, from down there, and I shrunk as a man in every way I could have imagined. I wanted to escape into a hole and die, and so, apparently, did my special purpose.

As he went through the procedure, I longed for death. I hated it so much. I hated every single moment of it with my whole being. He asked me at one point if I'd like to look at the screen and see what he was seeing, and I got mad at him for even bothering to ask such a foolish question. He saw the look on my face and quickly said, "Looks like you just want me to finish up as fast as I can?"

I grunted in a way that I intended to mean, "Yes, doctor, that's what I would prefer."

I remember thinking afterward that if they found out I had cancer (I didn't), and they needed to do that procedure again to save my life, that I would choose death. That's how much I hated it.

But honestly, as I look back, I don't know how painful it actually was. Probably not that painful. It certainly couldn't have been as painful as almost breaking my nose on that glass wall after my mega-float, but the suffering was so much more intense in this second story. The suffering wasn't limited to the procedure itself either. I remember going home afterward and just rolling around and moaning with the traumatic memory of it. So much suffering for what was probably a very small amount of actual pain.

. . . . .

So, what's the difference between these two stories? How could less pain create more suffering? Because pain is not synonymous with suffering. Suffering, as the Buddha taught, is the result of clinging to desire and aversion, not simply pain. Suffering is what happens when we desire something to be other than what it is. A person feels the sensation of pain, but that sensation is not suffering in and of itself. It is the emotional response to the pain that becomes suffering. The clinging to the aversion of pain is what brings the mental suffering, not the pain by itself.

This truth makes many of us feel uncomfortable. Saying that suffering is the result of our own attachment to our desires can sound like a dangerous idea—one that people could use to put the blame of suffering on the sick rather than the sickness, victims rather than abusers, the oppressed rather than the oppressor. And unfortunately, that sort of abuse of this truth can and has happened for millennia. In India, for example, thoughts like these have been used to justify and support oppressive caste systems that favor certain people over others. "If you suffer, it's your problem" is a potentially abusive and harmful justification of violence. The danger of a reframed and misused truth doesn't make it any less true though. Atomic bombs are a potentially devastating and violent use of atoms. Waterboarding is an oppressive use of water. This doesn't mean we can dispense with atoms or water.

The truth is that a person with no desire would have no capacity to suffer. One doesn't suffer while unconscious under a general anesthetic as the state of consciousness that includes desire goes off-line. Sure, pain can be inflicted upon someone from the outside, but pain is not the same thing as suffering. Pain is a physical sensation, but suffering (at least in the Buddhist sense) is a subjective experience.

This explains why there is still so much suffering in the world in the early twenty-first century, despite all of our technological advances and pain management capacities. It also explains why humans tend to suffer more than other animals. Plants suffer. Animals suffer. But nothing (that we know of) suffers to the extent that humans do. For instance, while there are other mammal species like dolphins, whales, and chimps that have shown signs of being aware of their own mortality and even mourning their dead, there aren't a whole lot of chimps out there wearing black for a year or going back to visit the graves of their deceased loved ones for decades. A dolphin suffers when her calf is killed by poachers, but a human can suffer by just worrying that someone might kill her child someday. Humans suffer more than other animals because humans cling to desire more than other animals. Not only do we desire to live but we desire to build, to conquer, to create, to imagine, to thrive. As Maslow's hierarchy of needs demonstrates, humans tend to find a whole new set of desires to pursue once they have fulfilled their current ones. Our suffering doesn't go away when our basic needs of food, shelter, or sex are met. Instead, we just find new things to desire. Relationships. Status. Power. Self-actualization. Spiritual enlightenment. Human desire is like a feedback loop. We want more and more and more, and as a result, we constantly find new ways to suffer.

Our penchant for suffering seems to be wired into our very DNA. We are all born into a cacophony of undifferentiated vibration and sensation. Before words, there is no way to box reality into conceptual categories like "somethings" or "someones" to be desired or to have aversions to. Here, before any distinctions can be made between a doctor or a nurse, a liberal or a conservative, black or white, rich or poor, naked or clothed, there is only the overwhelming and insignificant blur of sense without meaning. Still we cry. Why? Because even before desire becomes rooted in specific ideas and stories, desire still exists. We are born with and, in a way, *as* desire.

From the very beginning, we are unsatisfied with *THIS*, and so we imagine a *that*. Like the story of the Creator(s) in Genesis, we separate light from dark.[9] Desiring to be like gods, we parse, name, and judge reality into something we can understand and therefore control. Warmth is distinguished from cold. Milk from mother. Good from evil. Physics from theology. This splintering universe of construct, memory, perception, and language is created from every word we speak and every thought we think.

Our divine fiat: "Let there be suffering!"

We want *that*, not *THIS*. It seems to be built into our DNA as a species. *Life is suffering*.

We move from the dark into the light, and we suffer because we

9. It makes you wonder, doesn't it—whose image is made in whose?

miss the quiet peace of the dark. Then when the lights turn off, and it's time to go to sleep, we suffer because we are afraid of what the dark may take away from us. We can't wait to be older, and then we wish we were younger. We can't wait to graduate so life can truly begin, but then we can't wait to get a better job, a bigger house, or more free time. We want *that*, not *THIS*. *That* will finally make us happy. *That* will fill the existential void at the center of our being.

Riches.

Respect.

Fame.

Justice.

Security.

Heaven.

Nirvana.

A healthy, "typical" child.

Whatever it may be, it is always *that*. Not *THIS*. And even when we get *that*, it never quite satisfies like we want it to.

How is it possible for a being who lives on a sparkling blue planet with penguins and palm trees and trampolines to be anything but constantly overwhelmed with gratitude, love, and laughter? Why do we let so much life pass us by because we are coasting through its miracles on autopilot looking for something other than what is right in front of us? And what is it that we are looking for exactly? Something more interesting or wondrous than *THIS*? What could that possibly be? What do we think we would actually be satisfied with? Trees with blue leaves rather than green leaves? Money? For what? Fame? For who? Power? To do what exactly? Power to breathe more air? Hear something other than sound?

One need only look at the lives of the rich, famous, and powerful to see that the cycle of suffering is never externally solved. We're all aware on some level of the fallacy of the idea that when a person finally makes X amounts of dollars, or buys that new car, or finally signs that record contract, or gets a million followers on Instagram, that she is finally going to be perfectly happy and content for the rest of her life. But we chase the futile promises of these phantoms anyway. Until we can't anymore.

THE SPA
Part 2 (2012)

I turned the glorious shower off, wrapped my towel around my waist (well, a little higher than that so I wouldn't have to confront the truth that my belly now extended a bit beyond the towel line), and sauntered over to the steam room. There was an old, naked guy in there, but I hoped he wouldn't bother me if I kept my head down and kept quiet. I opened the door and was immediately inundated with that heavy, nostril-burning, eucalyptus-saturated air that is that prime steam room vibe I had been longing for. I disappeared into the steam, like an angsty gorilla in the mist. It felt good. I sat on that slippery, bacteria-ridden steam room bench, closed my eyes, and tried to pray. For the ten-thousandth time, I prayed that if God could hear me that He/She/It would help me. I was just so tired. Tired of the heaviness. Tired of the doubt. Tired of trying to create a god I could love.

How did I keep slipping back to this place in my head? After nearly losing my faith completely at that altar in 2009, I had experienced a bit of a personal revival. From the verge of a complete burnout in 2010 shortly after our first daughter, Amelie, was born, I had Googled "best spiritual retreats in the world" and found a silent meditation retreat in Assisi, Italy, the home of St. Francis of Assisi. In the hills that Francis used to preach to the animals, God came alive for me again. I had a mystical experience where God felt to me not to be a "something" to believe in or not believe in, but simply that which is. God became infinitely greater and more beautiful than any one religious tradition or people group could envision. He could not truly or accurately be thought of as a "he." In fact, he could not be truly or accurately thought of at all. Any conception of God would be an object of thought, just as idolatrous as any graven image or golden calf. God, as Infinity itself, could only be experienced directly within *THIS* moment. The world brimmed with glory. The universe became the very Word of God. God did not limit "himself" to a single sacred text or exclusive group of people. He/She/They/It was the All in All. The infinite Ground of Love and Being.

But in the months that followed my Assisi trip, I slowly began to fall back into old patterns of thought and behavior. In the humdrum of the daily grind, I found that the mystical glory of the world began to slowly fade into "normal" again. This frustrated me, and I tried to up my meditation game in an attempt to fix it. But it seemed like the harder I tried, the worse the problem got.

Now, here I was, two years later trying to pray in a steam room, worse off spiritually than I had been before Assisi! It felt like the core of my being was a tightly wound ball of suffering and contradiction. I didn't believe that God was a big scary "he" in the sky anymore, but for some reason, I still felt like I had to perform for him. I didn't believe in hell or think that God would be so petty as to be angry at me for my "sin," but I still found myself constantly repenting under my breath throughout the day. I wouldn't have said that I wasn't worthy of being loved, but I still didn't feel worthy of being loved.

As I tried to pray, it felt so futile. If there was a God, and he actually answered my prayer, why would he have chosen to answer mine over someone else's? If there really was some divine being out there that could hear and answer prayers, why would he only approve the request from the privileged, cisgender, fairly light-skinned, straight American dude having an existential crisis in a luxury spa and deny far more important petitions from Syria, Iraq, or one of the people chained up in some psychopath's basement at that very moment?

Entropy. Death. That's what really seemed to have the last word in this universe, not love. If God was as good as I had always believed and sang about, how could so much of his creation be so bad?

As I sat there, theologically homeless in that steam room, trying to pray to a God I wasn't sure existed, I felt hope slipping away. This wasn't working anymore. Oh well, I was feeling a bit overheated anyway after that long shower. I went to my locker, grabbed the plush, white robe and made my way to what would soon become the ground zero of the final deconstruction of my faith—the place where the most important *that* in my life would die to make room for *THIS*—otherwise known as the "relaxation lounge."

As I entered the relaxation lounge, I was greeted with the faint scent of essential oils and the soothing sounds of spa-appropriate radio.

There were four beige leather lounge chairs lined against the wall, all empty. On the left side of the room was a small table topped with packets of herbal tea and a clear plastic liquid dispenser filled with ice water and cucumber slices. I collapsed in one of the beige recliners, closed my eyes, and started to meditate. Meditation had been a big help for me through the last couple of years.

So I sat in that lounge chair focusing on my breath, hoping to feel something again. I don't know what I was hoping for exactly. Just something. Anything other than this. Nothing changed, though. The angst remained. I pulled my phone out of the pocket of the plush, white bathrobe, not feeling like meditating after all. Perhaps reading something inspiring might help.

Henri Nouwen? Richard Rohr? Eh, too Christian for my mood.

One way I'd recently been tinkering with that annoying theodicy equation in my head (*Omnipotent + All good + Omniscient + Sovereign = the Holocaust?*) was through the "all powerful" assumption. I really had been into some of the ideas from the "radical" or "weak God" theologies that people like John D. Caputo, Slavoj Žižek, or Peter Rollins wrote about. In this theology, God is not found as an all-powerful divine king or "Big Other" out there somewhere but as the insistence of a radical, material, political, and love-based faith to be experienced within and for this world. Here, God is found born in a manger, not dwelling in a heavenly palace. The Son of God was not a Caesar, conquering nations with chariots and horses, but a poor man, from an oppressed group of people, who was nailed to a cross, only to say, "My God, my God, why have you forsaken me?!" The God of radical theology is a small and weak God who is not found, seen, understood, or directly experienced as an object, but rather "found" in the loss of the conceptual idols that would turn God into a something that could be found. It was great stuff.

But I wasn't in the mood for that either. Honestly, something in all of this nuance and theological sophistication still just felt like some really good humanism trying to hold on to the word *God* for some reason. Humanism was great, but it couldn't explain what the hell we are all doing here. It didn't make sense of the universe for me. It may have given me some clever turns of phrase and a more interesting lens to interpret Bible stories through, but it didn't give me a God to worship or believe in. But why did I need that?

I needed to know the truth. I needed to know whether reality was good or bad. I needed to know how I could be okay. As lovely as radical theology, or universalism, or mysticism, or any other open-minded, openhearted theology may have been, none of it satisfied my deepest need to understand *THIS*. What are we doing here? Where did all of this come from? I could use the word *God* to describe a human experience of love, sure, but that experience was based in what? A meaningless Big Bang followed by innumerable chance collisions? Why bother with all of the God talk then?

No, I didn't feel like reading any theology. I didn't think it would help, and it all felt made up anyway. I couldn't meditate. I couldn't pray. What else was there?

For some reason, I suddenly recalled a show I'd been watching called *Homeland*, where one of the main characters converts to Islam. I felt a prick of curiosity.

In my years of attempting to craft a god that could allow me to continue being a worshipper of "God," I had learned many valuable lessons about spiritual practice and disciplines from various religions along the way. I learned how to wrestle with scriptures from the Jewish tradition; how to love my enemy from the Christian tradition; how to meditate from the Buddhists. I wondered if perhaps there might be some antidote to my individualistic, consumer-based, hyperrational American mind within the Islamic tradition.

As a Christian artist, I had traveled to countries where I had heard the calls to prayer and seen the devotion to righteousness and love of God that so many Islamic people have. I wondered if what I needed was a healthy dose of submission, of humility. Maybe there was some key in Islamic practice that could unlock something in my Western, reductionistic, individualistic mind. I tried to recall the words that the guy on *Homeland* had said while he knelt to the East to pray . . . It was something like, "Allahu achbar." I wasn't totally sure what that even meant, but I assumed it was some sort of praise to God. *Hell, I've got nothing else. I'm desperate. Might as well give it a shot.*

I got off the lounge chair and knelt down on the floor, too desperate to give a damn about who might come in and see me or what they might think.

I put my hands up to my ears, like the Caucasian TV actor had done, and bowed to the ground.

"*Allahu achbar*," I awkwardly pronounced, really trying to get that back-of-the-throat sound right.

I came back up, hands still up around my ears.

Allahu achhhhbar.

Was I overdoing the phlegmy sound thing?

Back down.

I continued this for a bit, up and down, up and down, until suddenly, something shifted in my perspective. It was as if I could suddenly see what was happening from a different angle, as though I were floating above my body in the room and seeing myself from a third-person perspective.

There he was, that sad and hollow frame of a man on his knees, trying desperately to hold on to his beliefs. So afraid. I felt sorry for him. This poor guy who spends so much of his life talking, writing, and singing about faith, hope, and love, all while his heart is empty. He has tried so desperately to craft a god worth believing in so that he can *say* that he believes in God and maintain some semblance of his life, but ironically, this effort to hold on is killing him.

This sudden awareness of the absurdity of the situation stopped me in my tracks. I quit trying to appropriate Islam for a moment and just knelt there. What if I just stopped trying to believe in God?

This question jump-started thirty years of well-honed defense mechanisms in my brain. I couldn't do that! I couldn't let go! It could ruin my life!

As an evangelical Christian kid, I was taught that our belief in God was the only thing that kept us from being like the murderers and prostitutes "out there." I was not quite as deluded as that anymore, but still, I didn't know what exactly would happen to my moral compass with God completely out of the equation. God was, and always had been, the source and foundation of all my ethical assumptions, aesthetic sensibility, and moral framework. For me to fully embrace an atheistic nihilism—that nothing had any inherent meaning, that the universe had no moral arc—was to throw myself into a completely new universe. What kind of person would I become? Would I care about people anymore?

I shouldn't think about that. I lowered my face to the floor again.

· · · · ·

It was as if I was a man in a rushing river, clutching tightly onto a branch. That branch was the only thing keeping me from the perilous unknown of the rapids' pull. I could feel my *Allahu akbars* falling into that same abyss that my words had in that chapel in 2009. There was nobody listening.

But what about Lisa? My bride. The love of my life. My first gift to her had been a navy blue, leather-bound Bible with her name engraved in the cover. I had underlined *our* verse in it: *Trust in the LORD with all your heart and lean not on your own understanding; in all your ways submit to him, and he will make your paths straight.* That was the foundation for everything in our lives and in our relationship. To lean on my own understanding right now would be to fall off the path entirely. What would happen to our marriage? Would I stay faithful to her? Would I resent the fact that I've only ever kissed one girl and just start sleeping with whoever will let me?

No! I couldn't let go!

Allahu akbar!

God, if you're there, please, help me here.

Allahu akbar!

Allahu akbar!

I could feel my hands slipping from the branch. It was out of my control.

What about Amelie? What about my friends? My parents? My career? Bloom? How would they feel about me losing my faith? They would be mortified, of course. I could lose all of them. My whole world could fall apart. Why am I even considering letting go? This is *God* I'm thinking about letting go of. The Daddy who was there for me even when my earthly daddy had failed me. My best friend, whose healing presence I had felt so strongly in that room as Lisa and I sang worship songs over my wounded parents' marriage. My source of grace and forgiveness when all I felt was shame. How many times had I sung of his faithfulness? How many hours had I spent studying his Word? How many tears had I shed in his presence? He had been the anchor that kept me safe in the storms of the chaos and pain of the world around me. How hard I had tried to keep my faith in him, to stay faithful to the one who I had believed was always faithful to me.

Allahu akbar

All . . .

I stopped.

It was as if my hands had grown numb and cold after so much clutching, and the muscles just weren't obeying anymore.

My clenched fist continued to weaken, as I realized the futility of my internal debate. I couldn't unsee what I'd seen. I couldn't unexperience what I had experienced. I couldn't create a faith I didn't have.

For a terrifying moment, I took my focus off the branch and braved a glance at the river—its torrents swollen and fierce. What was this river exactly? The movement of evolution and life and chaos and entropy? Everything that's brought me to this point? I wondered . . .

Could it be possible that this river might be . . . good?

It occurred to me that if there was really anything or anyone real or worthwhile remaining in my belief structures—any form of any god worth having faith in—certainly He/She/It/They would be secure enough to handle my lack of belief. Was I so narcissistic as to think that my personal doubts were going to throw the entire universe off its course? Any god worth his salt would surely have enough self-confidence to put up with people who didn't believe the "correct" things about him, right? I'd long ago let go of the cartoonish, vengeful, angry Santa Claus figure in the sky who was always watching, always needing us to believe the right things. I, who am not even invisible by the way, certainly wouldn't care much if I found out some dude didn't believe I existed. Was God less self-realized as a being than I? Why did I feel like ultimate love would be threatened by or dependent on my own personal belief constructs?

Maybe John Mayer was onto something when he wrote, "Belief is a beautiful armor but makes for the heaviest sword." I've never had a server at a restaurant question my beliefs about human thirst after I asked for ice water. Bankers don't often hold inquisitions for the depositors of checks in order to determine whether or not their client's beliefs about the tenets of capitalism are orthodox or heretical. I have had a lot of preachers ask me about my beliefs about God though. Seems to me the word *belief* is used when people are expected to enact the opposite of trust—to grit their teeth, shut their mind down, and swallow.

Maybe this wrestle in me to have to *believe* wasn't actually about God, but about me and the culture that I come from. Maybe the wrestle was simply me being afraid to leave the flock that I found my identity and safety within.

Maybe this river is good . . .

It echoed again in the quiet center of my heart. I felt that ever-present longing for truth. For freedom. I felt a sincere desire to seek, know, and love reality—whatever that is. I was there on my knees because that is where the journey toward truth had brought me. The river, whatever it was, had brought me here, and I could see now that I was simply afraid of where the river would take me next. That was the source of my suffering. That's why I had been trying so hard to hold on. I had fooled myself into thinking that holding on to my faith had been an expression of love and desire for truth, but it was actually an act of fear—fear of the unknown, of the river, and what she might take from me if I let go.

I let go.

I took a breath.

I stood up. Alone.

Nobody was there? Nobody was there. What a strange feeling to think that there wasn't anybody listening to my thoughts but me. Nobody was judging me. I didn't have to perform. I didn't have to measure up to anything. I was just a guy standing alone in a spa in a bathrobe. How wonderful was that?

My chest felt lighter. My mind clearer.

I suddenly remembered that my brother, David, was in town. I had avoided hanging out with him because of my existential angst spiral, but now I realized that I wanted to see him. I got dressed, left the relaxation lounge, and headed outside to call him. On my way out, I saw the young woman at the front desk again. *THIS* young woman at the front desk. A fellow human with all of her own suffering and dreams and desires and possibly even her own occasional existential crises. I no longer had any mythical metaphysical constructs of divine calling or purpose that made me *need* to be nice to her. I didn't need to manifest any divine love for her to experience the kingdom of God. And I didn't even have to repent under my breath for those blasphemous thoughts. I was just standing there. She was just standing there. That was all. And it was enough.

I smiled at her, said thank you, and wished her a good day. And I really meant it.

When God Is *THIS*

When God is *THIS*, God is here.
When God is *that*, God is dead.
Do your idols make you happy, my love?
If they do, then play with them with a full heart.
Worship them. Lift your arms to the sky and dance with them.
Dress them and paint their fingernails.
Give them as many heads or eyeballs as you'd like.
But when the paint begins to peel or the brass begins to tarnish
Feel free to throw them into the flames of Love
And peer into the reflection of your own Divine Face.

WALKING MY DOG IN THE RAIN

A Parable (PART 2)

I've run into some issues. It's been a really stormy season around here, and as a result, my resolve to stop walking my dog in the rain has really taken a pummeling. I think I finally realized I didn't have the willpower on my own to stop. I tried and tried, but it seemed like every time we were out there on overcast days, and I was staring at those rain clouds, willing it not to rain, it wouldn't work. It rained anyway, and there I was with my dog. In the rain. That disgusting wet-dog smell. Being fiscally irresponsible. And hating both myself and my dog for it.

I decided to get some help. I enrolled myself in some online positive-thinking courses that I am optimistic about. I feel like I've been making some good internal progress and am pretty sure my willpower is increasing, as we've been getting a lot less rain than we were last week. I've also been studying the power of habit and the law of attraction. I'm learning that if I can visualize what it's like to not walk my dog in the rain, I'll be able to actualize an ability to stop. I can see now that my problem was that I was too focused on the negative aspects of walking my dog in the rain rather than positive aspects of me as a human being who doesn't need to step outside every time there is even the slightest chance of a sprinkle. When I can see that, I can believe I am complete and whole as I am, and that I don't have to walk my dog in the rain after all.

Again, I think all of this is working pretty well so far because I've had a really good stretch of sunny days lately. It's been so sunny that I barely even thought about walking my dog in the rain. I really am feeling good about myself with all of this, but don't want to let my guard down, because we all know that pride cometh before the fall.

Suffering Is the Attachment to Desire

67

To Catch the Fly

W hen we, through reflection or therapy, probe into what we think of as our problem (that extra drink, white fragility, too much porn, etc.), we almost always can find a layer in which our problem is really our solution. We swallow the cat to catch the bird to catch the spider to catch the fly. Or in my case, the theological problem I was trying to solve was really a solution for shame and anger, which was really a solution for daddy issues, which were really a solution for that fundamental sense of not-okayness at the core of my being.

This is not to say that the problems that stack up aren't real and troubling issues. Whiteness (the racial construct and all that goes along with it, not the color of people's skin) really does create systems of racism and oppression for people of color. Patriarchy really does lead to more rape, body shame, and unjust pay scales. That drug addiction really did destroy that marriage. Some theology really is inherently more beneficial to human thriving than other theology. The problems we feel are real demand our attention. But until we begin to look at the mechanism by which all of the problems continue to mount and build on other problems, we will never be fundamentally okay. We will always be scratching at our poison ivy—temporarily relieving some discomfort but creating new problems in the process.

Our suffering is never fundamentally about what she said or what he did or that I don't have enough money in my bank account this month. The source of our suffering is never anywhere but inside our own minds. Our suffering is always and only the result of our clinging to our desire for *THIS* to be *that*. Anthony de Mello, a Jesuit priest and psychotherapist, said it like this: "If you look carefully, you will see that there is one thing and only one thing that causes unhappiness. The name of that thing is attachment.[10] What is an attachment? An emotional state of clinging caused by the belief that without some particular thing or some person you cannot be happy."[11]

This is an absolutely necessary realization for your freedom, and one that many of us are reluctant to accept, and partly for good reason—it's an easy truth to misunderstand and misuse. For that reason, I would like to remind you once more of the dangers of abusing this truth. Imagine someone telling a widow who recently lost her husband that her suffering was her own problem because it was just a result of her attachment to her desires. That would be an inhumane twisting of this truth, and one that misses the point entirely. After all, to assume that someone else *should* experience anything other than what they are experiencing is to be attached to something other than *THIS*. Sometimes loving *THIS* looks like fully experiencing anger and rage. Sometimes loving *THIS* looks like grief. When you understand that loving *THIS* is not the same thing as apathetic resignation, you will also be able to see that there is no reason for you to try to judge the internal experience of someone else. You have no idea how deeply they are clinging to the pain that they are experiencing, and therefore have no right to tell them what freedom should look like for them in their circumstances. The truth that our suffering is a result of clinging to *that* rather than loving *THIS* is never a truth to impose on others, but rather an infinite ocean within yourself that you are free to swim in if you so desire. It's as simple as letting go.

As we will see in the third Noble Truth, when we see *that* and learn to love *THIS* as it is, with all of its warts and tiaras, something amazing can happen: The feedback loop of suffering can actually dissipate and we can become more like our wise, old grandparents—the sun, the moon, and the trees. You see, trees don't waste a lot of energy clinging to their desires or aversions, trying to live in an imaginary reality that isn't *THIS*.

10. It's an important distinction that the second Noble Truth teaches that our attachment to desire is the cause of suffering and not the desire itself. Desire is natural and important. Without desire, we wouldn't eat. We need desire, but when we get attached to our desire, we suffer.

11. Anthony de Mello, *The Way to Love: Meditations for Life*, Kindle ed. (New York: Random House LLC, 2011).

6. Riding the Ox Home

THE THIRD NOBLE TRUTH

The End of Clinging Is the End of Suffering

Myths

"Chop wood, carry water."
—Zen saying

A fter my experience of letting go of God in the spa, I felt free, alive, and openhearted again, sort of like I felt after Assisi. Only this time, I didn't have to try to live up to anything. I didn't have to repent under my breath anymore. I didn't have to strive to be anything other than who I was in any given moment. And ironically, the result of this was that all of the elevated "spiritual" feelings I had been seeking my whole life were suddenly available freely and without strings. It was as if I traded my old, tattered idea of God for the glorious reality of what I had loved when I loved God. This had nothing to do with the specific content of my new myth of atheism, but simply because of my changed relationship to *THIS*.

The word *myth* is not used here as an equivalent to saying stories that are simply not factually accurate. Myths are big stories that contain and explain other stories. For instance, if you could show an iPhone to someone from ancient Greece, they would have a fundamentally different experience of that story than an Apple technician would. Whether one experiences that object as an unfathomable magic crystal radiating the divine light of the gods from its belly or the second-generation iPhone X, an advanced telecommunication device, depends entirely on which myths you inhabit. All of our relationships, religions, nations, money, war, law, medicine, art, technology, philosophy, and science[12] are rooted in some sort of mythic structure that allows us to make sense of the world and gives us a sense of identity within it.

---

12. While many people today consider science the antidote to myth, the practice of science is still a human meaning-making, and therefore "mythic," endeavor (as defined above). As the modern age has demonstrated, rational and scientific thought can help us build and destroy with tremendous power, but it cannot, by itself, determine what or how we should build or destroy. Science cannot, by itself, offer any sort of moral, spiritual, or aesthetic guidance to humanity. For that, we need myths. Without myth, there would be no possible meaning derived from experimentation.

Scientific materialism is a myth. Modernity is a myth. Post-modernity is a myth. Theism is a myth. Atheism is a myth.[13] Again, myths aren't "false stories"; they are big, meta-stories that help us interpret and make meaning from the world around us. If you didn't have myth, you wouldn't have any meaning, any language, any concepts. This is why it can be hard to recognize the extent of how your own myths color your thoughts, feelings, and fundamental experiences of reality—trying to conceive of how you conceive is sort of like trying to see your own eyeballs.

Our most fundamental assumptions about existence—the mean-ing of life, where we come from, what we are doing here, whether we are real or illusory, material or divine, magical or mundane, fragile or immortal—all of our baseline assumptions about what *THIS* is, who we are and how we should act, come from the stories that we tell and the myths that we experience the telling of those stories through. You may think that "you" "live" "on" "Earth," a "planet" "in" "the" "universe." But all of that is story. You live in story. You are story.

Because of the power of story and myth, people are willing to work most of their waking hours for an imaginary construct called a cor-poration in trade for an imaginary value called money and pay a high percentage of that imaginary construct to another imaginary entity called the United States of America. One of the reasons our myths are so powerful is that they not only offer us a sense of meaning but an identity and feeling of belonging.

I am the oldest of four children from the Gungor household. Rob, David, Lissa, and I were all raised with the same parents in the same places. We had a lot of the same teachers. Same friends. Same vaca-tions. A lot of similar experiences overall. And wouldn't you know it? None of us are devoted practitioners of Zoroastrianism. I think this is for the same reason that there is a fairly strong statistical correlation be-tween the number of Canaanite Baal worshippers in any given society and whether or not that given society is ancient Canaan. It's because our belief systems are the result of where and when we were born. Our myths, and therefore self-identities, are given to us by our cultural context and social bonds. As such, those stories become central to our

13. This might be objectionable to some atheists or others who might want to pride them-selves on being myth-free, but atheism or scientific naturalism are still ways of rendering an otherwise unintelligible cacophony that is the universe into an understandable, and therefore "mythic" construct, even if that construct uses words like "chaos," "natural selection," or any other human constructs to create or destroy meaning.

feeling of identity. We get attached to them (in fact, as we will explore soon, what we think of as ourselves *are* those attachments). We die for these stories. We kill for them.

Most of us don't pay attention to how closely our identity is tied to the stories we tell of the universe. Westerners are often notoriously bad about this, thinking of themselves as objective arbiters of rationality and truth. But this isn't how human beings work.

Puerto Rico is 0.13 percent Muslim while 99.8 percent of Afghanistan is Muslim. This is not because every individual in these countries just coincidentally happened to come to the exact same fact-based, rational conclusions about the doctrines of Islam, but because they, like all of us, just want to be loved. We want our friends and family to like us. We want to be safe, to belong, and our beliefs are part of that. Or as Sartre said, "If I became a philosopher, if I have so keenly sought this fame for which I'm still waiting, it's all been to seduce women basically."

Our meaning-making stories are fundamentally and intrinsically tied to our sense of identity, and as such, we have all sorts of evolutionary mechanisms in play in our brains and society that reward us for friendly acquiescence within the tribe and punish us for going against the grain. We may love our saviors and revolutionaries in the rearview mirror, but tend to nail them to crosses when they dare to actually show up in the present because messing with our stories is messing with us. As the spiritual teacher A. H. Almaas wrote, "Becoming free of the fixation of any perspective is the same as becoming free of the self."[14]

In saying all of this, I'm not trying to put all stories on equal footing. Recognizing that the Apple technician's view of the iPhone is every bit as steeped in the mythic stories of her culture as the ancient Greek person's or anyone else's interpretation and experience of the iPhone would be is not to say that all myths are equally valid or useful, but simply that there is no such thing as an objective point of view. The perspectives that feel objective to us feel that way because that's the mythic framework from which we are seeing. The Apple technician's perspective may feel more objective to us than those myths of distant cultures, but that is only because we are so thoroughly entrenched in the worlds that our own stories have created.

14. A. H. Almaas, *Runaway Realization: Living a Life of Ceaseless Discovery* (Boulder, CO: Shambhala, 2014).

Every day that the earth spins around the sun is experienced in billions of different ways. Today is both heaven and hell on earth, depending on which stories you are inhabiting. One person's delicacy is another's reality TV–show dare. One person's god is another person's devil. One person's Trump is another person's . . . Trump. All human language, beliefs, traditions, religions, myths, and stories are simply different perspectives and experiences within the same one reality. The mystic Baba Ram Dass said, "All of us are on the same journey; we just have different metaphors."

We may all be ultimately part of the same Oneness and on the same journey, but our differing viewpoints and metaphors make for very different individual experiences of that Oneness and journey. Everything that you think imprisons you—it's just a story. And when you can see that, you are free.

This is the reason why I could feel so liberated after both my mystical experience in Assisi and my donned atheism of the luxury spa. The freedom and spiritual awakening had very little to do with the specific contents of my theological or metaphysical assumptions about reality (which, as an atheist, was that everything is essentially random, pointless chaos). In fact, atheism as a story that made sense of the universe would be something I would also find the need to let go of eventually, but that wasn't nearly as difficult or painful because I wasn't emotionally attached to it in the way that I was to my belief in God. For this reason, I usually have very little concern about the specifics of people's belief systems.

The stories that *THIS* is experienced through are different for everyone. A person can be free whether she is an atheist, agnostic, spiritual but not religious, religious but not spiritual, Catholic, Protestant, Eastern Orthodox, Buddhist, Muslim, Jewish, Hindu, or anything else, as long as the stories that she inhabits do not become her prison. Sometimes, for some people, *THIS* is named Christ, Allah, or Krishna. Other times, *THIS* is thought of as matter, reality, or the universe. Any name we give it is a story, and all stories have shelf lives. Some can go a whole lifetime being best friends with a bearded man in the sky. Good for them! Others need a change of scenery. That is perfectly fine, too.

I met a girl recently whose deconstruction story was nearly the opposite of mine. Her parents were atheists and had raised her to be a good secular humanist who didn't believe in those silly fairy tales and superstitions that religion had fooled and brainwashed so many into believing. Being an atheist was an integral part of her tribal identity, and in her journey, she had found great freedom in letting go of that identity-forming myth and opening herself up to the mystery beyond the scientific method.

It seems to me that how we inhabit our myths is generally more important than the specific dogmas, language, and metaphors that these myths use. For instance, I'd much rather attend a service at a church that preached that sacrificing goats was an acceptable act of worship but didn't actually sacrifice any goats themselves than attend the service of a church whose belief statement included the phrase "all goat sacrifice is sin," but who just went ahead and whopped a few billies and nannies on the head during the offertory announcements. This is because how we live through our stories is more important than the words we use to describe those stories.

The words we use are rarely accurate or truthful in describing what we *really* believe anyway. Most people who say they believe in a literal hell spend an awful lot of time *not* running through the streets in a panic warning everyone that they need to repent or they will burn alive for eternity. They spend a lot of money on things that are not evangelistic outreaches that could possibly spare people from an endless existence of conscious torment. So are those people really bad people with no compassion for humanity, or is it that deep down, they know that their beliefs about hell couldn't possibly be true?

In saying that the way we inhabit our myths is more important than the specific contents of those myths, I'm not saying that the contents don't matter. They do because they have an influence on how we live. If our orthodoxy (correct belief) is sexist, our orthopraxy (correct practice) is likely to be as well.

But as much as the contents of one's beliefs do matter, it's far more important that you avoid actually *believing* in your beliefs.

I say that playfully,[15] but in my experience and perspective, the most destructive acts of religion come from the fundamentalism of people

---

15. Obviously, some level of belief is necessary to function in the world. If I didn't believe milkshakes were less healthy for me than water, I would weigh significantly more than I do.

taking their beliefs too seriously, especially when those beliefs can lead to the harm of others. Every biblical literalist has the verse in Leviticus in their Bible that says that gay people should be put to death, but very few of them take it seriously. Every atheistic scientific materialist believes that human life is a product of a natural universe and is no more intrinsically meaningful or valuable than the meaning or value one projects into it, but I've never met an atheist who treats human life as though it is actually inherently worthless. When we forget that our beliefs (or lack thereof) are just combinations of words, and our conceptual positions concretize into absolute and literal Truth, we get in trouble.

It's one thing to think that your kid is the best kid in the whole world. It's another thing to *believe* that your kid is the best kid in the whole world. Putting drawings on refrigerators is one thing, but if someone is writing daily, exasperated letters to news outlets, bewildered as to why little Johnny's finger paintings aren't yet in art museums is another.

It's easy to recognize and condemn the fundamentalism of the extremists we disagree with—those who fly planes into buildings, strap bombs to their chests, or hold up signs with hate speech printed on them. It's not so easy to recognize our own attachments to our own myths. And while not all myths are equal—all attachment to any myth creates suffering. We need stories, but when an open faith devolves into a closed fundamentalism, we become even more imprisoned by that which we hoped could set us free.

Regardless of how beautiful the story or belief may be that you are clinging to, the truth is that as soon as your fingernails are burrowed into it with attachment, the story becomes only about your own ego. "Love is patient, love is kind," when *believed* with a tight fist rather than an open hand, becomes "I am a loving person, and therefore better than all of you." When God is a noun, God is an idol. Even a huge and all-inclusive story about Oneness or nondual realization can become a way of trying to extend the ego out to infinity when one gets attached to those words or stories as though they were something more than words or stories. It is even possible to get attached to the idea of nonattachment! I once read of a monk who experienced that and consequently shifted his spiritual practice to working on becoming more attached to the world. Regardless of how cleverly the ego attaches to these stories or how good or true the stories may be, that attachment will always result in suffering, and letting go of that attachment will always result in freedom. Freedom is not some other place for one to someday finally arrive at or achieve, but simply the full reality of here and now, of *THIS*, without the clinging to our attachment of trying to be somewhere or someone else. For most of us on a spiritual path, we will move in and out of these states and feelings of okayness and not-okayness. For me, I experienced tremendous freedom and breakthrough in both Assisi and the spa, but then as time went on, a new challenge or life circumstance would present yet another opportunity to let go of something. Like the layers of an onion, our attachments to our desires and aversions go deep into our very sense of self, and it is only by the grace of the river herself, often in the form of suffering, that we can peel those layers away until the true, undivided self of *THIS* is experienced in its fullness.

Let There Be

I n the Hebrew Scriptures, the universe begins with speech.
"Let there be light."
That's how it goes.
Nothing exists until something is said.

Light (2014)

S "he has physical characteristics consistent with Down syndrome."

The nurse's voice trembled as if she were handing us a
death sentence. Had I known then what I know now, I could
have smiled at the melodrama of someone delivering the news of our
newborn daughter Lucette's twenty-first chromosome with the emotional timbre one might use to deliver news of an imminent, species-annihi-
lating asteroid collision with Earth. If I had known then how much joy
my Lulu would bring to our lives; if I had known how precious every
moment of life is, regardless of the number of chromosomes it builds
its tissue with; if I had known that nurse's dire-sounding pronounce-
ment was simply a limited description of one aspect of the unique and
marvelous attributes of our new little princess, I could have responded to
the nurse by saying something like, "That's fantastic news! Thank you.
We are so lucky."

But I didn't say that. I didn't say anything at all. The most I could
do at that time was nod helplessly, tears flowing down my cheeks.

As we received the news of my daughter's diagnosis in that
hospital room, I was not okay with the *THIS* that had suddenly and
unexpectedly presented itself. The bottom of the world dropped
out, and I was in a free fall. I couldn't believe what I was hearing.
This couldn't really be happening. Not to us. We weren't responsible
enough to handle something like this. Lisa and I were flighty, bohemian
musicians who had a hard-enough time keeping our lawn and our
firstborn alive! Trying to effectively parent one child in our chaotic
world of airports, buses, vans, and grimy, phallically adorned green
rooms was already a stretch for us, and I was already worried about

trying to add a second kid into our mess. A second kid with special needs? Nope. I knew I couldn't do that. I was already at my limit. So as I took in the news of Lucette's Down syndrome, I watched an entire world of *that* crumble before my eyes.

I looked at my wife Lisa. She looked stronger than I felt. Of course, I could have figured as much. Unlike myself, Lisa's first thoughts in life are not always about her own needs and convenience. For instance, when we went to Africa together once with a nonprofit organization that helped children, Lisa cut her ankle on a rock one day while playing in the forest with some of the children. Had that happened to me, I would have immediately put everything and everyone out of my head except what would have been my new and single-pointed life mission—retreat to a clean environment in order to sterilize and secure the wound. Lisa, however, barely noticed. When I, aghast, pointed out the blood trickling down her foot, she shrugged it off and grabbed a nearby stick to wipe the blood off with. *A stick? In a Ugandan forest?* We had to get a bunch of shots just to fly there, and I'm pretty sure none of those immunizations were intended for cleaning open wounds with random detritus from the forest. I mean, I know a stick in Uganda probably doesn't have more bacteria on it than a stick in Los Angeles, but as a bit of a germaphobe, I knew that stick was most likely covered in parasitic, flesh-eating bacteria with AIDS.

I yelled at her as though she were about to step off of a cliff, "*Stop! What are you doing?!*"

At that point, she realized that it probably wasn't the most sanitary way of attending to her cut and laughed and moved her attention right back to the children. You see, Lisa isn't a person who tends to think so much or so quickly of her own needs as I do. And so, yes, she looked sad after the nurse delivered the news of our new baby having Down syndrome, but I'm pretty sure it was mostly because she was worried about the health of the baby. I was mostly worried about myself.

And then the soul-crushing thought entered my mind, "Is this my fault?"

My heart sank further into despair. I searched my memory and recalled a night, around the time the baby had been conceived, that I had taken a couple "Colorado gummy bears." Did I do this?

Time became a blur. People coming and going. Talk of surgery. All I wanted to do was Google "Can marijuana consumption cause Down syndrome pregnancy?" I eventually got the opportunity to leave the room. I pulled out my phone. No, there was no correlation between marijuana usage and higher rates of Down syndrome pregnancies. Thank the gods. Still, I couldn't shake the feeling that this all was somehow my fault. My world was collapsing. The hospital walls were closing in around me, and I was suffocating. I escaped outside to get some fresh air and walked around the block for a while. The thoughts were relentless.

Why is this happening?
What are our options here?
I don't want a baby with special needs.
I didn't sign up for this. I can't handle this. We can't handle this.

I called my sister, Lissa, who is a Christian. She told me that God knit this baby in her mother's womb and that it's going to be okay. While my atheism had gradually morphed into more of an evolved version of my earlier mysticism in the couple years that had passed since my experience at the spa (my experience in Assisi ended up being too significant to completely dismiss), I still didn't believe in any sort of divine being that knits babies together in wombs.

Eventually, I walked my collapsing self back into the flame-engulfed world of the hospital room. I was told the baby needed two heart surgeries, one of which would have to happen immediately. They would go in through her back and somehow fix part of this tiny, fragile baby's heart.

"Maybe that will be the end of it," I thought, and immediately hated myself for it. Lisa was crying. She was terrified that the surgery wouldn't work. I was terrified that it would. What was wrong with me? I felt ashamed.

I looked at Lisa—the warrior queen who had now survived two human beings growing in, then coming out of her own body like an *Aliens* movie. She was scared but strong. Seeing her made me wonder if maybe it was somehow going to be okay. Something in me knew that we would end up loving this baby girl just as much as our first, but I was so afraid. Afraid she would die. Afraid she wouldn't, and that I would. Afraid that this would ruin our marriage. Our family. Our career. I was a man who had dreams. I had a vision for my future. I had all of these thoughts and feelings about what my life was supposed to look like, and certainly none of them resembled anything like this! But where had those thoughts come from? Was our yet unnamed, hours-old baby girl, who was whisked away and still off being poked and prodded by the doctors, really any intrinsically less valuable than any other life? Almond-shaped eyes are still eyes, aren't they? Crooked pinky fingers are still pinky fingers. Hell, my pinky fingers are crooked, too.

I walked over to Lisa and looked deeply into those brilliant blue eyes I fell in love with when I first saw them fifteen years before. I never would have imagined being in this moment with that girl with the cute gray skirt and the magical blue eyes. Now those eyes were full of tears. So were mine. Both of us were absolutely terrified. But I wanted her to know that I saw her, was with her. I couldn't do this, but maybe *we* could. I didn't know who or what "God" may be, but in that moment at the hospital bed, I could once again feel how whatever the creative force behind and within it all—that knits babies together in wombs— was present. This baby was still a baby. Not just a baby. *Our* baby. I gently laid my hands on Lisa's belly, and those old words, that psalm I had memorized as a child, began to flow out of my mouth as a sort of prayer for this new baby girl of ours.

"For you created her inmost being; you knit her together in her mother's womb. I praise you because she is fearfully and wonderfully made."

Afterwards, we held each other and cried. We cried for the pain of it all. For the beauty of it all. And in that moment, something in our hearts opened and we began to let go into that timeless, inconceivable, ineffable *THIS* that knits together galaxies and spinning blue planets and mothers' wombs and almond eyes. Similarly to what happened in Assisi, and at the spa, something significant inside of me broke out of its chains and became free. From that moment, our stories about Down syndrome, about what a "good" or "healthy" life looks like, about our baby girl, all began to shift radically. What I thought was a wound became my healing. And not just mine.

My dad and I hadn't had a great relationship at the time of

Lucette's birth. I had told him about my letting go of belief, and as a pastor and deeply Christian man, that understandably upset him. The philosophical elephant in the room had sometimes made it difficult to try to talk about "normal" things. Neither he nor I are prone to loquacious small talk. But when Lucie was born, we found a common ground on which to meet. My daughter. His granddaughter. She needed a family's love and support, and we were both willing to put aside our differences for the task. He was there in the hospital with us. He cried with us. He told us how much this baby girl would be loved. And how I loved him. And in my time as a dad, I've begun to understand my own father more and have been able to see how much he always loved me. Even after his worst mistakes and deepest shame, he always came back for us.

Today, that chunky four-year-old with the crooked pinkies is one of my favorite human beings on earth, and that's not only because she's my daughter. Lu's favorite song is "Happy Birthday." She loves it. She sings it all day, often even in the morning as she is waking up with her low, groggy, sleep voice: ". . . appy Birday to Looolooo . . . appy birday to you . . ." I think she likes the song so much not because of its compositional structure or lyrical depth but because she associates it with parties. Lu loves to party. Come to our living room, turn off all of the lights except for the dance light that was our family's best purchase decision of all time, crank up the right music, and look around for the shirtless, twerking toddler holding a sandwich in one hand and a packet of apple sauce (pronounced "saw" in Lu language) in the other—that'll be Lu, a human being more full of life, love, passion, and presence than almost anyone I know. Her life is not a burden for anyone. It's a gift.

Today, I can see how closed-hearted, ignorant, and even bigoted I was when Lulu was born. It wasn't that I hated or pitied people with Down syndrome (DS) or anything; I just didn't know anybody who had it. I only knew what our culture had told me about DS. I only knew what I experienced from society—the look on the nurse's face, the absence of people with DS in our media, the quickly shrinking DS population due to the extremely high abortion rates. In our society, this baby girl's life was seen as "less than." It was assumed to be nothing but a miserable life of suffering. Nothing could be further from the truth. Sure, there are hard days and complications. She is human after all. But our society teaches us a weird myth about how life is supposed to look. The top of the societal ladder is straight, white, male, cisgender, and able-bodied. Baby girl with Down syndrome? Sorry, that's *way* down the ladder. And though I never would have thought that I bought into those sorts of societal lies, my emotional roller coaster in the hospital had proved otherwise.

The stories we tell are the reality we experience, and from my limited frame of reference steeped in all of the myths of twenty-first-century American life, I could only see a condition that threatened my personal pursuit of happiness. My experience of the world was limited to the small, destructive stories from which I was viewing Lucette (and everything and everyone else). In these flawed stories, I could only see failed expectations and changes in hoped-for circumstances. It didn't take long though until she helped me to see the light. And that's what we ended up naming her—Lucette—it means "light."

Karma

T he high peaks of freedom that I experienced in the wake of letting go in Assisi, the spa, and the hospital were all eventually followed by valleys of suffering in one way or another. In Assisi, my mystical high wore off eventually, and even though I still had the souvenirs of my experience in the form of language, metaphor, and memory, I had once again gotten lost in the weeds of belief. In the spa, I experienced tremendous and lasting freedom from shame and the need to comprehend the incomprehensible, but, as you might expect, my social web and sense of tribal belonging completely fell to pieces, leaving a giant existential hole in my sense of self. I found out firsthand that being an atheist really is not the best career move for a Christian musician. Our career went into the toilet. We went into debt. We lost our management. We had money stolen from us. People said untrue and hurtful things about us. We had a good friend die. All of this was happening just as Lucie was born.

Lucie, who not only needed all of the attention and money that any newborn needs but also heart surgeries and extensive therapy. How could we travel? Traveling was how we made a living. We were terrified. And we felt more alone than ever because this was all happening simultaneously with a bunch of church drama where one of my closest friends, whom I had hired to help pastor the church we had started, tried to kick us out of our own church. So we didn't really have our church family to walk alongside us through any of the pain we were experiencing. We felt alone and depressed. We tried to escape the drama of Denver by leaving for Los Angeles, but the house buyer backed out on the day of closing, and we ended up having to move in with my parents in Oklahoma.

We just couldn't get a breath. Life had devolved into pure chaos. I lost some of the most important relationships in my life. I felt betrayed. Gigs kept canceling. Lisa and I were fighting a lot. We had this new baby girl with special needs who we didn't know how we would be able to raise, and our sweet little Amelie was getting far too little of our attention in all of the mess.

As I look back at that period of time now, I can't help but laugh and shake my head. It was insane. It hurt like hell, but somehow, we made it through. What I can see now is that all of that suffering was simply the river (karma[16]) doing what she does: washing away that which I thought would be my salvation. Washing away all of the *that* while at the same time offering the ever-present and infinite *THIS*.

The thing about suffering is that at a certain point, it takes the ability to cling to desire right out of you. At a certain point, you lose the storyline. Perspective gets jumbled so that up is no longer up, down is no longer down, and all that's left is *THIS* moment.

Here's what that looked like for me:

I would feel completely overwhelmed and depressed and had no desire to get out of bed. But then Amelie would wake up and tell me she was hungry, and I had to look at *THIS*, my daughter needing food, or *that*, my own narratives about what my life was supposed to look like. And I'd just have to get out of bed and pour the goddamn Cheerios.

It looked like me feeling sad a lot. I would weep out of fear and shame and pity for myself. And then eventually the tears would stop flowing. And I would take a shower and watch a movie. Not because I acquired the wisdom of always being present in the here and now, but simply because the *that* had run its course, and there was nothing else to do.

What it looked like was that I was mad a lot. I would pound my steering wheel with my fist and say the worst things I could think of at the top of my lungs. And then the light would turn green, and I'd keep driving.

This is life. It does what it does. It turns here and bends there. It drops you off a cliff and into a thorny bush, and then it offers you a rose. What happened for me to make it through that time was that life simply went on and so much of the *that* which held me hostage simply withered up and died of old age or maybe starvation. All things die at

16. By karma, I simply mean the unfolding *action* or *doing* of the All.

some point. I would be stressed out about the *that* of how far behind
Lucie was in her crawling or fine motor skills or any of the other line
items on the therapist's scorecard, but then it would be time to rock her
to sleep and I would sing lullabies to her, and she would coo and gurgle
while my crooked pinky finger curled up around hers, and *that* story
would fall away into the staggering glory of *THIS* moment. Here, in
THIS, all the tests and rankings in the world that told me what my baby
girl was supposed to be didn't matter in the slightest.

Then another career door would slam shut in our face, and I would
feel impotent as a provider for my family. Then I'd sit in the corner and
play my guitar as I watched my three girls playing and dancing together.
I'd watch Amelie's blue eyes beam as she twirled around her little sister,
who despite not being able to crawl, could headbang like a rock star
in the '90s. I'd marvel at Lisa's innocent, childlike ability to play and
laugh with the girls despite all of the pain I knew she was experiencing.
As I watched them, I would realize just a little more how beautiful life
is regardless of how many chromosomes, positive magazine articles, or
well-paying gigs it has.

What happened to get us through the hardest time of our lives is the
river simply continued to flow. I'd feel despondent. I'd read a chapter in
a book by Karen Armstrong and realize that some people don't have a
firm idea of who or what God may be, but they still have a meaningful
spiritual practice in their life. I'd be angry at American Christianity and
write a snarky song. Then I would meditate a little, and let that anger
go, allowing my heart to open to the God I didn't really believe or not
believe in. And I'd get depressed again, but then have to let go to get
out of bed again. And again. And again. The river did what she does.
Life moved on.

The river would offer a conversation with a friend. A transcendent
sushi dinner. Another meditation retreat. Another career disappoint-
ment. A new friend. A failed idea. A podcast. I'd discover an audiobook
by a guy named Ram Dass and watch how the ideas within it resonated
with my own experience.

Step by step. Moment by moment. A slow and steady surrender.
Attachment by attachment, constriction by constriction, myth by
myth—slowly, but surely, one breath at a time, She continued to flow, to

cleanse, to ravish, to heal. It felt as though She was teaching me how to loosen my grip, over and over again. It felt as though She was allowing me to become more and more free—free of who I thought I was supposed to be, free of the life I thought I was supposed to have. This river is ruthless in her grace. No shortcuts, it flows as it will. There's nothing you or I can do about it. Fight it to the degree that you want to suffer. After that, there is always surrender.

Shaman (2016)

I met my first shaman at a progressive Christian festival. He spoke to the winds and the trees and did everything I hoped a shaman would do. I participated in a ceremony with him that involved hand drums and chanting and all sorts of aesthetics that I would have considered dangerously demonic when I was younger. We ended the ceremony by silently listening for the great Spirit to whisper a word to us. If and when we heard it, we were to come up and write whatever the word was on a stone of our choosing with a black Sharpie. The black Sharpie didn't seem all that shaman-like, but I rolled with it anyway. I had lived in Los Angeles for a couple years at that point, and was getting more comfortable with woo—the native religion of LA. But also, I had felt something shifting inside of me again through the last several months and was in a very open place spiritually. I had been listening to a lot of Ram Dass and Alan Watts. I was meditating a lot. I was deeply interested in mysticism again, and having a lot of spiritual experiences that were a bit reminiscent of how things were in the afterglow of my mystical experiences in Assisi. But this time, there was something a bit different about all of it. My thirty-five-year-old ego was a bit quieter than my thirty-year-old one had been. I had been through a lot the last few years, and my hands were getting used to not always clenching my stories so tightly. I had recently told Lisa that it felt like something significant was about to happen in my spiritual journey. I didn't know what exactly, but I could feel the seas beginning to part.

I sat in the shaman's ceremony, closing my eyes, listening for any word that the "Spirit" might whisper (even if the Spirit was nothing but my own unconscious mind). Sure enough, the word *flow* began to repeat in my mind over and over. I tried for a moment to dismiss it, thinking that I must have just thought of it on my own. But it kept repeating. So I figured I'd go with that one. I walked to the table, picked out the rock that grabbed my attention, and wrote the word *flow* across it with the shaman's black Sharpie.

To be honest, it was a bit underwhelming. I simply went on with my day. Then, that night after we played, I was invited to go to a house where the shaman would be, and apparently, he had grown some very special fungi that he might be willing to use for another spiritual ceremony. Now this was interesting!

I had never taken mushrooms or any other illegal substance before. (Not counting Colorado gummies, because, well, it was Colorado.) I had always been suspicious of people's "spiritual experiences" while on some sort of substance. It just seemed to me that such an experience could not be trusted. But in all of my Ram Dass studies, I had learned a great deal about psilocybin (the active psychological ingredient in "magic" mushrooms) and had become very curious about it. The reports had shown no harm whatsoever to the brain (except in fringe cases involving schizophrenia or other mental illnesses), unlike what I had been raised to believe in the "say no to drugs" era. In fact, the few studies that were out there reported overwhelmingly positive responses for most people exposed to mushrooms, including increased happiness, creativity, and feelings of love and connection and a decrease in negative feelings like depression or anxiety for time periods up to fourteen months for a single dose. Also, I had learned enough about the brain from my friend Science Mike by that point to know that everything that we experience in "sobriety" is really a hallucination that our brain is creating for itself anyway. No human experience should be trusted to the point of infallibility. So I said yes.

We pulled up to the house, and my heart was racing. Was I actually going to do this? Was this stupid? Would I get arrested? I was nervous, but there was something under all of that, something that knew that this was about to happen and that it was going to be okay. Once inside, the shaman explained to the few of us there that if we wanted to do this, it was to be engaged as a spiritual sacrament. This was not a party. It was a ceremony. These plants were not drugs. They were teachers.

In hearing how serious this was going to be, some of the people in the room opted out, deciding that it wasn't right for them at that moment. Others of us stayed, heeding the call. The shaman asked us to set an intention. I knew mine immediately.

At the spa, I had decided to not believe in God, but by my own definition, God was not a *something* to believe in or not believe in. Choosing to not believe was, in a weird way, a method of believing my own definition of God. I had already known that God was to be experienced, not believed in, but still I had tried to believe in him. In the past several months, I had begun to experience "God" in a deeper way again, but I still needed the quotation marks. My go-to fundamental myth about reality was still essentially postmodern, scientific materialism with an openness that I might be wrong. That night, I wanted to know—do I need quotation marks around God? Is there anything out there beyond what the senses can perceive or the scientists can theorize? Is it silly to call "God" a "Thou" rather than simply an "it" (the universe)? I wanted a direct experience of God in some way. A voice. An image. A realization. I didn't care. I just wanted to be free forever of any remaining shadow of needing to figure out what I meant by "God."

We spoke our intentions to the shaman, and then he administered the sacraments. They tasted earthy. My heart began to race. I sat down in my normal meditation pose—legs crossed, index finger against my thumb, paying attention to my breath. The shaman told me that I looked like I was trying to do something. "Maybe try just lying down." He smiled. I lay down, hoping to see the face of God. Instead, I became the gaze of God looking back at my Self.

The next five or six hours is difficult to translate into words, but it was as if I had been wandering through a forest my whole life, looking at the trees all around me, trying to figure out where I was exactly— what kind of forest was this? How big was it? Who planted it? But as I lay down and melted into the cosmos, it was as though the camera suddenly zoomed back, allowing me to see that *I*, the true I, was not *someone* wandering around the forest—I was the forest itself. I was no longer a *someone* in the river, choosing to flow with the current or not, I was the flow of the river herself. Later that morning, while walking around in contemplation of the experience I had with the shaman, I put my hand in my pocket and felt the Sharpie-marked stone I had completely forgotten about. In that moment, I saw so clearly how it all went together. Everything in my experience to this point and every experience I would ever have in the future went hand-in-hand with *THIS* moment. Before I knew what *flow* meant, before I had fully melted into the empty awareness of its ever-present ubiquity, it had been whispered into my soul from the great Spirit, my very Self. I pulled the stone out of my pocket, looked at the word, and wept at the beauty of it All.

And finally, we can now come back to the period at the end of the sentence, and why the realization of the nondual, interconnectedness of All is tied to our freedom.

One Becomes Two

Sub Ek (All Is One)—Neem Karoli Baba

I t's all one. This is something that mystics, sages, yogis, and psychedelic users have been saying for millennia. It's one of those phrases that probably doesn't mean much until you've really experienced it for yourself, and then it means everything. You know, like, "Someday, you're not going to care so much about cooties" or "Parenting is difficult." The nondual unity of everything and everyone is an idea that you might see expressed in fortune cookies, on the walls of yoga studios, or in the pages of cheesy, new-age, self-help books, and so it can be easy to dismiss it as sentimental woo, or to find it interesting but impractical, like the knowledge that there are approximately two trillion galaxies in the visible universe. It may be true and even impressive, but still, what are we going to do about these gas prices?

In my journey, "It's all one" evolved from being a meaningless statement to a heretical idea to a fascinating possibility to an inspiring truth to a life-changing reality to simply *THIS*. In the months leading up to the shaman's ceremonies, I had felt my heart softening to a place I hadn't ever experienced before. I had studied a lot of Buddhism, Hinduism, and Taoism, and the ideas resonated so deeply with me. I wrote songs about all being One. I thought back to Assisi and remembered how God (ultimate reality), was not experienced somewhere else. He/She/It was closer than my own breath. For twenty years, I had been asking the *big questions* about the world "out there." What was all of this? Was God real? Was there any meaning to life? But until I laid back on that shaman's floor, I had never fully turned that deconstruction laser beam on itself. I had never fully questioned the questioner. I had never fully let go of the person who thought he needed to let go. I had always looked through the eyes of ego, looking for something real "out there" in the world. But this experience placed me, the observer, in a different enough frame of reference that it made me realize for the first time in an experiential way how fundamentally my experience is connected to my perspective. There was no real, separate me to be a prisoner, other than the stories in my head.

From that point onward, something deep and fundamental had changed in the way I experienced the world. Rather than only seeing through the ego, as though I was separate from all of *that* out there, the sense of "I" melted into the All.

To be clear, it is not that any experience of ego disappeared entirely. Without some physical and even emotional sense of where one's skin ends and the outer world begins, it becomes impossible to function in the world (as I experienced after my "mega-float"). But my ego was taken off the throne of the universe. It was almost like the camera of my observer zoomed out far enough to reveal that there were *cameras shooting a scene*. I always felt like I had been directly viewing the world. Now I saw firsthand that there was always a mechanism involved in the viewing, and that realization changed my life.[17] The effects of the psilocybin wore off, but I couldn't unsee what I had seen. From then on, I could no longer believe or feel that my experience of the world was objective or disconnected from anything else. Sure, I still had questions about God, about reality, but I could now see that all of those questions were mechanisms of the ego. Those were questions stemming from some pattern in my brain that wanted to make sure my mom still loved me and my dad was proud of me. It was just my mammal brain wanting to ensure a good place in the social pack so that it could be assured of its own safety and ability to procreate. It was all just stories.

What I saw and couldn't unsee was that here and now, in *THIS*, I am always totally free. In *THIS*, I am unafraid, unshackled, and grounded in the All in which I am. This freedom doesn't mean that I experience nothing but happiness or excitement all of the time. I still experience pain, sadness, anger, and the full gamut of human emotions that make this life so fascinating and full, but I am no longer imprisoned by these feelings. I experience them like breath. There is *THIS* inhale.

---

17. I'm sure there are many who would question the truthfulness or reliability of this realization, as my mind was in an altered state when I experienced it. And that's fine. I don't feel a need to prove anything to anyone. But the way I see it, whether a person needs a rocket ship, a book, a tribal narrative, or a tab of LSD to realize the earth is round, the earth is still round.

THIS exhale. I don't cling to the in-breath when it is time for the out-breath. Nor do I cling to the memory of yesterday's breath or worry about the certainty of tomorrow's. In the same way, there is *THIS* sadness. *THIS* joy. *THIS* bliss. *THIS* aggravation. It comes. It goes. I experience it as fully as my mind is capable of experiencing it in that moment, but the experience does not get stuck under my fingernails like it used to. I used to cling to my life, to my stories, to offense, and worry and doubt. Now I see how that sort of attachment to desire only results in suffering, so I have no more desire to cling to these feelings than to hold an angry wasp in my hand. Better to just let it pass. When I do not cling, but simply remain in and as *THIS* very moment, I am free. And if you have "ears to hear," so are you.

This freedom is not just an idea or way of seeing, nor is it a way of disassociating with reality. Rather it is an ever-deepening embodiment of letting go into the fullness of *I am*. It is the letting go of who we think we are and simply being fully present and open in our bodies' experience of right here and right now. As natural as this freedom may be, most of us do not feel free. This is because life has evolved in such a way that the experience of feeling separate is necessary for survival. After all, if I felt no physical separation from that tiger who wants to eat me, why would I run? If I didn't *feel* that my life and the lives of those I love were more important to tend to than any other pattern of energy in the universe, why would I choose to feed my child as opposed to that flock of birds who are probably hungry as well? Some sort of intrinsic feeling of distinction from our environment and each other is essential for both our survival and our thriving. But unity is not the same as uniformity.

Assuming "sameness" can be very destructive, especially in contexts that involve oppression or injustice. For instance, our so-called "color-blind" justice system in America assumes a level playing field for all people and therefore ignores the racial bias inherent in every level and arena of the entire system, from police to juries to judges to court clerks to law schools. The result of this is an institutional racism that makes a black man six times more likely to go to jail than a white man charged with the same crime. When black people are convicted, they're sentenced to approximately 20 percent longer prison terms and are

38 percent more likely to be sentenced to death than white people are for the same crime. And that's just the justice system. Our entire world is full of injustice for people of color, women, LGBTQIA+, the elderly and handicapped, people with differing abilities, mental illnesses, body shapes, and on and on it goes. To assume that we are all the same can erase very real and important distinctions that are not only matters of fairness, kindness, and community but sometimes even of life and death.

There is no unity or "oneness" without difference. The vast differences within the universe all work together like the different systems, organs, and tissues of a single body. And if we lose track of either the differences or the underlying unity that allows those differences to exist, we lose our way. One needn't shove pizza up one's anus simply because it is part of the same digestive tract as one's mouth.

Consider the following scenario: Imagine, if you will, that I invite you to come over to my home for a private concert. When you arrive, I tell you that I would like to play for you a selected portion of a beautiful piece of music that has changed my life. You happily agree. I sit down at the piano, crack my knuckles, place my hands on the keys and take a deep breath. I close my eyes. I play a single note. Middle C.

It rings out, filling the room with its sonorously lonely presence. I take my hand off the piano. I stand and bow.

You look confused but choose to smile politely. Noting your lack of enthusiasm, I'm confused as well.

"Well, what do you think?" I ask, expectantly.

"Well. That was nice, but is that all of it?"

"No. The full piece of music is a Bach sonata, but like I said, this was just a *selected* portion. The note C does occur many times in the piece."

This is how so many of us interact with the world around us—as though the universe really is a set of separate things and events that could all exist on their own—like individual notes in a piece of music or a wave captured into a jar. We think that our politics could exist without their politics. We think that our in-group could be happy without their out-group even though our sense of *us* is defined entirely by not being *them*. Music is not merely the sum of its individual notes but the experience of all of those notes relating to each other within rhythm, timbre, and silence. In the same way, ultimate reality is not merely the sum of a bunch of separate things and events. Reality is also the fundamental unity and relationship within all of the differences that allow us to have particular experiences within that Oneness.

Oneness and difference go together like light and dark, space and matter, up and down. In the same way that everything you've ever seen or heard from a computer has been made entirely of 1s and 0s, everything you see in the universe is composed of the peaks and troughs of vibrations—off/on, life/death, back/front, self/other, yin/yang.

This universe is an interconnected infinity of unified differences. And just like our alien friend Marge from earlier in the book, what we see and experience within that infinity depends on how and from where we look at it. Whether the period at the end of the sentence is seen as a banal dot on a page or the expressed fullness of an infinite and liberated *THIS* is simply a matter of perspective. Whether we experience reality as a disjointed, chaotic mess of suffering or a seamless, glorious symphony of unified differences depends entirely on what sorts of stories we are telling.

Story is what turns One into two, unity into difference. Story looks at an ocean and draws a line around part of its movement and says, "Let there be wave!"

Story is a prism through which a single beam of uniform sunlight becomes a rainbow of different colors. It can transform an amorphous ball of Play-Doh into a house, or a world, or a thousand tiny Buddhas.

Story is everything, and everything is story.

Stories are the way of drawing imaginary lines across an otherwise seamless and, as my favorite philosopher Alan Watts used to say, "wiggly" reality—the only way that we can exist as a someone with a question to be asked or answered. But when these stories are *believed*, we often mistake the model of reality in our heads for the thing itself. Because when you get down all the way to the source or essence of reality *before* One is made two, there really isn't anything that can be said that is fundamentally "true" or "real." Down there at the foundations of the world, there is only *THIS*—ineffable, unquantifiable, unthinkable isness that is beyond language, concept, or story. This reality is not "physical" or "spiritual" or both or neither. It is not "God" or "Creation" or both or neither. It is not "Form" or "Void" or both or neither. Perhaps the most we can meaningfully say about *THIS* is *neti, neti.* (Not this, not that.)

All language, all religion, all concept or understanding of that ultimate reality is an idol[18] at best. As soon as you can think of it, it is not *IT.*

"The Tao that can be told is not the eternal true Tao." This is the first line in the *Tao Te Ching*, which is, ironically, a book that *tells* us about the Tao! This is the perfect way to begin the *Tao Te Ching* though because the power of all of the wisdom, truth, and beauty within its pages would be degraded if the reader were to take the words too seriously and think that the Tao was something that could be adequately thought of or written about in a book.

Our stories and language will always be based on a fundamental illusion that one thing could ever really be separate from another. It is out of this illusion that ideas like ego, free will, and good and evil are born. It is out of this illusion that we get religion and philosophy and science and all the rest of it. Having these sorts of stories in play is absolutely necessary to human life and flourishing. We can't entirely escape or avoid all stories, because like we have seen, we are made of stories and there would be no possible perspective from which to experience anything without them. But if we want to be free, we must let go of our attachment to these stories. Here, in this free and loving awareness, there is nowhere to go but back to our original Face. There is nobody to try to be other than the manifested All. There is nothing else to cling to, nowhere else to be, nobody else to impress. Just *THIS.*

---

18. I use the word *idol* here in the same way as I do in the rest of the book—in the Judeo-Christian sense of a physically or conceptually crafted object used to turn infinity into something controllable, understandable, and ownable. Whether it is a literal golden calf or the idea of an infinite, mysterious being, as soon as one can possess it, it is an idol. For more on this, I would recommend reading Peter Rollins's *The Idolatry of God: Breaking Our Addiction to Certainty and Satisfaction* (Brentwood, TN: Howard Books, 2013).

WALKING MY DOG IN THE RAIN

A Parable (Part 3)

I woke up last night to the sound of thunder. I quickly threw on a robe and ran outside with my dog to get a good look at things so that I wouldn't have to walk him in the rain. It was raining really hard. The streets outside my apartment were flooding, and then I saw something absolutely shocking. I saw a woman . . . *walking her dog in the rain.*

I'm not even kidding. It was the strangest thing I ever saw. It was the middle of the night. Nobody was around but her and her golden-doodle. They were just walking, right there in the middle of an intense rainstorm, like it was no big deal. In fact, both she and her dog seemed perfectly happy. They splashed through the puddles on the sidewalk without a care in the world. She never fell to her knees, weeping. She never yelled at the dog for how smelly he most likely was. From the looks of things, she didn't even seem to care that it was raining. I was shocked. I was offended. And then two ideas occurred to me.

First, I realized that walking one's dog in the rain is not the end of the world. I mean, as surprising as that may sound, I saw with my own eyes how okay this woman was with her choices, and it made me feel that maybe I'd gotten a little too serious about my dog-walking choices. Maybe walking your dog in the rain is a perfectly acceptable thing to do if you want to do it. I'm not sure why I ever cared so much. Who really cares if someone walks his dog in the rain?! If that's what one wants to do, I think one should be free to do it! In fact, now that I think of it, it doesn't really matter in the long run if you and your dog smell like wet dog for a little while. You'll dry. If your clothes get wet, they'll dry. If they get ruined, you can always get new ones. I guess it took a long time for me to realize this, but I'm really glad that I finally did.

This first realization was obviously a big moment for me, but not nearly as earth-shattering as the realization that followed. The second thing I realized in seeing that woman with her dog in the rain was that I don't even have a fucking dog.

Letting Go of Yourself

W ho, beloved, do you think you are? That question is the root of the Problem underlying all the problems.

Under all of the:

I'm not lovable enough

I'm not good enough

I don't know enough

. . . there is the idea that you are a small and separate somebody who is supposed to look, feel, think, and behave in a certain way. But I have good news for you, friend—you, the real You, is already fully realized, completely perfect.

But . . . (your ego argues)

I'm an addict.

Or

I'm a pervert.

Or

I'm such an angry person.

Or

I'm such a fearful person.

You are no such thing. You are the All expressed in story that includes experiences of anger and fear and the rest of it. But you are not those things. Nor are you a person who needs to try to not be those things. That idealized version of yourself in your head that you "should" be living up to is a mirage. It is an illusion. It's a phantom given to you by your society in order to identify, understand, and control you. That ideal version of you in your mind that you're always striving to be—you know, the one whose body fat percentage is "perfect," or who nobody ever speaks poorly of, or who doesn't fly off the handle when her mother-in-law makes that facial expression, or who is prettier, smarter, and harder-working, or who has no interest in walking his dog in the rain—that person is an illusion. Like my friend Hillary McBride once said, "You've never seen your own face. You've only seen the face your world has reflected back at you." This face that you think you are supposed to look like is not your true face. It never will be. And it doesn't need to be. This phantom you that the world has painted in your mind is an illusion. It is a maze of expectations and assumptions with no exit. It's a piano concerto written with notes that aren't even on the piano. It's futility. It's suffering.

This isn't to say that a person cannot grow or change—experiencing less extreme anger or not harming themselves or others by living according to the stories of their addictions. On the contrary, people are change. What are human beings, after all, but an ever-moving and shifting pattern of energy? But the idea that by sheer effort and willpower, one can transcend the Problem of one's ego and become a "better person" is simply an exercise in futility. A knife cannot sharpen itself. You cannot be anyone other than who you are in this very moment, and you don't need to be. In this very moment, there is nothing that is missing. Nothing that is lacking. Nothing that is imperfect or ugly. It is only when we leave *THIS* perfection for the illusion of those other stories, where we are incomplete somebodies who need *that* to complete or fulfill us, that our experience goes off the rails into creating suffering for ourselves and others.

I think most of us focus so hard on changing rather than simply and mindfully being. If you desire to be a more loving person, for instance, you won't do yourself any favors by getting caught up in the story of you *not* being a loving person. What often happens when we cling to our aversions of *THIS* ("I wish I were more loving") is that our clinging becomes a fixation, which becomes the self-reinforcing loop that strengthens the undesirable behavior that we are trying to escape in the first place. Like St. Paul wrote in the Epistle to the Romans, "For I do not do the good I want to do, but the evil I do not want to do—this I keep on doing."

The first step in AA's 12-step program is honesty—admitting powerlessness in the face of addiction. Why do they do this? Because they recognize that the idea of that all-sufficient ego that can just theoretically summon up the willpower to say no to another drink is an illusion and that putting one's hope in that illusion actually only gives the Problem that much more power.

This clinging to futility, these loops of unsolvable stories, are the stuff egos are made of. The ego is that sense that I am a separate somebody from everything and everyone else. It is that wound at the center of our being that feels fundamentally not-okay. It is the clinging to desire that creates the wheel of desire upon desire upon desire, that endless cycle of futility that creates so much suffering in the world. The ego is not a *thing*. It is a function of the mind that is often experienced as a constriction of muscles, a feeling in a human body when story conflicts with story.

I am no more an ego that exists apart from the rest of the universe than I am a floating pair of flexed butt cheeks that have somehow been metaphysically disconnected from the rest of reality. The ego is how my brain overcompensates for the wounds that I have been dealt.

I didn't feel loved by my mommy, so I want to make a lot of money and have somebody notice me.

Or . . .

I felt unsafe as a child, so I must be the only person who can take care of myself.

The ego is the result of a human organism's desire to be permanent. It is a coping mechanism and a clever way for an organism to survive and procreate. Our evolved fear of death gets expressed as the story of a permanent, real, and consistent "self" that can have free will and make decisions and not simply be at the mercy of the gods or the wind. These ego stories can infuse our bodies with confidence and zeal that make it easier to survive and build civilizations, but the stories are illusions nonetheless. Helpful illusions. Until they aren't.

Who you think you are is just stories conflicting with other stories. In other words, *you actually don't even have a fucking dog.*

Fred was convinced that he had a problem with walking his dog in the rain even though he doesn't have a dog, just as the spiritual seeker is convinced that she has an ego problem even though "she" doesn't even have an ego as she thinks of it. She only enacts an ego experience moment to moment because she desires *that* rather than *THIS.*

The irony for both Fred, the phantom dog walker, and the spiritual seeker is that the source of their anxiety is precisely their desire to become free of their anxiety. They both want to be better. They both want to transcend that which doesn't exist. They both are fully engaged in futility. Fred takes classes and takes credit for making progress when the weather cooperates with his desires. The spiritual seeker meditates or reads the Bible for hours on end and then thinks she is making progress when she feels less "carnal" or more loving for a time. Fred seeks freedom by desiring to not be someone who walks his dog in the rain. The spiritual seeker longs to be spiritual by being "more" than she is in this moment. But what is the "more" that the spiritual seeker is searching for? Connection with God? She already has it. She already is it. The only thing keeping her from this realization and experience is her belief that she has to achieve or protect it somehow.

For so many of us, our biggest problem is actually that we think there is a problem. We try to resolve this perceived problem of desire by increasing our desire. This desire clinging to desire clinging to desire creates a wheel of suffering that we attach a false identity story to. The only way to escape this vicious cycle of desire and suffering is to let go of the wheel altogether.

You, beloved, are not a small, separate *something* that exists over and against a bunch of other *somethings*. You are the river. You are the whole works, being and doing and spinning stories like a million flashing sunbeams on the surface of a lake. All of the problems and solutions are simply movements within Yourself.

Dear friend, striving to solve your ego Problem of not-okayness by trying to be something or someone other than *THIS* is as futile as you constantly pushing your feet down to hold the earth in its orbit around the sun. There's nothing you can do to make yourself *better* because what you think of as you doesn't really exist. There's nothing you can do to make your ego permanent, immortal, or consistent. All of that is a dream within a dream—a happening swirling around an infinite number of happenings, none of which are intrinsically separated from each other. You are the same Music as the period at the end of the sentence. You are the same Ocean as the airplanes, hotels, coffee shops, and living rooms it was typed in. You are the author and reader of this book; you're its printing, its impact, its being forgotten, and its eventual disintegration back into the earth. You are *THIS* moment, the Alpha and Omega, beginning and end. Be who and what you want to be, here and now. It is You who are doing none of this and doing all of it. You have no "free will"[19] but for your one Supreme Free Will that is doing it all in the one timeless Now of the current's flow. And sure, you are even that illusory ego that thinks it has the Problem. So, walk the dog in the rain, or don't, but I dare you to look down at that leash you're holding and see if there's anything actually attached to it other than the stories in your mind.

19. The idea of "free will" is a construct built upon an assumption of a "me" who is separate from the All.

I Am

D id you forget who you were for a moment there, my Self?

Do you think you are simply the sum of a million little accidents?

A finite set of tubes, skin, blood, bones, and goo?

What a story!

What an adventure!

Next time, if you get caught in that dream within a dream and you want to remember,

Just lean in and I'll whisper your name.

"*I Am.*"

7. Forgetting the Ox

THE FOURTH NOBLE TRUTH
The Way

Becoming Free

*"Truly I tell you, unless some-
one is born again, they cannot
see the kingdom of God."*
—JESUS

nlightenment. Nirvana. Moksha. Freedom.
Realization. Salvation. Union. Satori. Samadhi.
The Kingdom of Heaven. Call it what you like,
but it's real and almost entirely missing from the
Western imagination. The language isn't missing—I grew
up talking about salvation all the time. We were not only
"saved," meaning that we were on God's good side and the
ones who would get to dwell with him for all eternity, but
we were "being saved" as well. This meant that we were
being purified and made more like Christ while we awaited
his final return. In other words, salvation was always about
something other than *THIS*. We would be fully saved
someday if . . .

In the same way, people in the West have taken the word
enlightenment and used it in ways that the ancient traditions
never intended. For a Hindu person, to be enlightened
is to have seen through the illusion of separateness and
experienced union with the divine. Immanuel Kant's famous
essay "Answering the Question: What is Enlightenment?"
more accurately defines enlightenment in the eyes of
Western individualism—thinking for oneself rather than
simply following another's direction. In more contemporary
language, the term *woke*, a popular slang word used to
denote someone who is awake or enlightened, has nothing
to do with waking up to the nondual nature of ultimate
reality, but instead is about becoming more aware of the
important, relative truths of social and racial justice.

Ancient terms like *awake* or *enlightened* are so distant from our collective consciousness in the West, that we can't even begin to distinguish the difference between the unity of ultimate reality that transcends story and the particulars of the relative reality of our stories. In other words, we've fundamentally lost sight of our own seeing.

Even before my spa episode, as a "progressive Christian," words like "salvation" or the "Kingdom of God" had become weak clichés in my ears. They were essentially metaphors for healthy living, and the sort of language that Jesus would use, like needing to be "born again," had frankly become a little melodramatic. Jesus went around talking about how the sort of life he was inviting us into would cost us everything. It was like a pearl of great price for which you had to sell all of your possessions. Being born again required surrendering your life, even to death. This language made more sense when I was a fundamentalist evangelical Christian, where I might have to become a martyr in the end-times while battling the antichrist or something. But after becoming "enlightened" to Western secular individualism and progressive ideologies that no longer interpreted the Bible literally, all of this "you must be born again" nonsense was a bit extreme and embarrassing.

And then I took magic mushrooms and was born again.

And now, I can see not only what the hell Jesus was talking about, but why he would use such extreme language.

Enlightenment—or nirvana, the Kingdom of God, etc.—is not a pot of gold at the end of the rainbow. So many of us "spiritual people" are, like the apostle Paul, trying to "finish the race," as though spirituality was a sport and salvation was the trophy we get at the end. Whether our prize is everlasting bliss with a bunch of virgins, strumming a harp in mansions of glory with driveways paved of gold, ruling the universe with Christ for all eternity, escaping the karmic wheel of birth and death, or transcending the ego into that blissful state of nonattached, nonduality—we want to figure out how we can attain it. We buy the books. We attend the conferences. We wear special clothes and skip meals and scour through old, boring sacred texts. We kneel, pray, and meditate for hours at a time. We overlook broken and violent religious systems, with their manipulative altar calls, racist and patriarchal power structures, child-molesting priesthoods, scientifically dubious ideas, or oppressive control mechanisms, hoping that if we persevere, we will eventually win. We will eventually get the gold star, the cookie at the bottom of the jar, the "well done, good and faithful servant."

What most of us are often actually looking for when we seek our spiritual prize—enlightenment, realization, salvation, or the like—is for the reality of this moment to be something other than what it is. We don't want to be *THIS*. We want to be *that*. We don't want to have *THIS*. We want to have *that*. We don't want *THIS* moment here and now, but rather some other imaginary "better" one that would make our vaporous ego shadows into permanent realities. But if that's your game, I have news for you, friend. There is no pot of gold at the end of that rainbow. There is only *THIS*.

By that, I certainly don't mean the same thing as people often mean when they say something like "This life is all there is." Or "Nothing exists that we can't see." When I say that *THIS* is all there is, I mean that if you did happen to find yourself singing with the angels in Heaven someday, what could that possibly be other than *THIS*? In other words, where can you experience anything other than right here and right now? If and when that happens, it will be *THIS*. Until it happens, it remains as an illusory *that*. There is nothing real that is not *THIS*, including enlightenment. Like Ramana Maharshi said, "It is false to speak of realization. What is there to realize? The real is as it is always. We are not creating anything new or achieving something which we did not have before." When you fully see through the illusion of *that*, you will see that even the illusions we create and the ego games we play are ultimately really still *THIS*— still the river experiencing itself. Awareness of nondual oneness and distortions of awareness of nondual oneness are both still part of nondual oneness. Ignorance of the nondual is also the nondual. There's no escaping it. You can't be anything but the fullness of the All expressed as you are here and now.

Still, all paths are not the same. Ramana Maharshi quotes are powerful for a reason. He did seem to live in a way that was more "realized" or "enlightened" than most people, even as that realization led him to denounce the idea of realization. So how does one move forward on the spiritual path, becoming more free, more alive, and awake? Surely, there is more to it than the dissolution of the ego and one's sense of separateness? After all, just because I (this particular organism) have been able to experience the freedom from attachment, and therefore suffering, the same will not necessarily be true for those around me. And if we truly are all connected as One, then none of us is truly free until all of us are free. A man does not stick his hand out of a jail cell only to forget about the rest of his body.

It is for this reason that the process of becoming free must continue beyond any individual's personal awakening to *THIS*. One only need look at the lives of countless spiritual gurus who talk the talk of having seen the light, only then to use their "spiritual enlightenment" in ways that end up oppressing or duping others. Sexism, racism, ableism, ageism, and any other sort of bigotry can still lurk in the shadows and patterns of a mind that has let go of its own sense of separateness and suffering. As such, attaining nondual awareness is not the be-all and end-all for the journey of a spiritual person who is not limited by the selfishness of only *their own* freedom, but rather is caught up in the loving work of the freedom for all living beings.

As Ken Wilber writes about in his book, *The Religion of Tomorrow*,[20] the spiritual path cannot only be about "waking up" or becoming enlightened to ultimate reality, because that experience will still be processed through the stories, perspectives, and shadows of the awakened person. Waking up is about coming to see the illusion of separation. It is the cessation of the false self that causes us to suffer and to strive. It is about seeing ultimate reality with a clear and ungrasping mind. Wilber argues that "waking up" must be accompanied by "growing up" and "cleaning up" in order to be healthy and holistic.

Growing up is about dealing with those fundamental mythic structures and points of view through which our state of being is lived. Our worldview determines whether we interpret the all-pervading light that we may see in our deep meditative state as God, an angel, a bodhisattva, an alien invasion, or a firing of neurons. An awakened perspective can still be embodied in a person whose view of the world is entrenched in authoritarianism, exclusivity, superstition, xenophobia, or bigotry.

Wilber points out how the East has often focused much more energy on waking up, and therefore often has better practices and philosophies toward that end than we do in the West. For all of their waking up, however, they have often left out important aspects of growing up that have ultimately hindered their spiritual progress and health. Many in India, for instance, have woken up to the nondual *isness* of reality but remain in harmful caste systems that value certain people over others.

Conversely, in the West, we have collectively done a lot more growing up with some of these sorts of social justice issues—the feminist movement, civil rights, scientific inquiry, equality, etc. Of course, we still have a long way to go in all of these areas, but at the helm of Western moral and social development, we are often further along in "growing up" issues like this than many other places in the world. As far

20. Ken Wilber, *The Religion of Tomorrow: A Vision for the Future of the Great Traditions—More Inclusive, More Comprehensive, More Complete* (Boulder, CO: Shambhala, 2017).

as waking up, however, the West is almost entirely asleep. As far as academia and power systems are concerned, the movement towards waking up to ultimate reality is not even present in our awareness.

As Wilber argues, a healthy spirituality would do well to include progress in waking up (realization of ultimate truth), growing up (maturity in relative truth), cleaning up (psychological shadow work), and showing up (compassion and activism).

Spiritual maturity takes time, energy, and practice.

In the fourth and final of the Noble Truths in Buddhism, Siddhārtha Gautama laid out his eightfold path for reaching nirvana, the cessation of suffering—right views, intention, speech, action, livelihood, effort, mindfulness, and concentration. Obviously, much has been written about all of this, and the specific traditions of Buddhism differ greatly in their approach, perspectives, and emphasis on all of it. For the purposes of this book, this fourth and final section will focus on exploring what I have found to be helpful pathways for experiencing deeper and deeper levels of freedom and enlightenment where life is lived to the fullest—not imprisoned by suffering, not blinded by illusion, but fully present, content, and awake.

But it is important to realize that in talking about the Way, we are not talking about a list of things that one has to do or believe in order to achieve enlightenment, as though enlightenment was some sort of a badge of honor or trophy to be won so that the ego feels better about itself.

In 2017, I received an email from a twenty-year-old from Missouri who told me he was enlightened, and he thought that from following my work, I might be too, unless I was just bopping in and out of temporary states and experiences of realization. I was intrigued. He came and spent a few days at my house with me. He smoked a lot of weed. He was into astrology. He told me that he wouldn't be surprised if Donald Trump was enlightened and just screwing around. The kid made me laugh, and I really liked him, but occasionally I would notice there was something about the way he talked about enlightenment that elicited some friction within me.

I questioned him about what he thought enlightenment was, and why he would keep calling himself enlightened. Wouldn't making a point of calling yourself enlightened be *believing* that you are a small and separate *self* that can be enlightened? From my reading and experience, most people who seemed to be truly enlightened didn't often go around emailing people, dubbing themselves as enlightened. Still, how could I know if this guy was actually enlightened or full of shit? He talked about reality in a way that sounded enlightened to me, using language like "Light of Light," "Infinite Joke," "Being-Consciousness-Bliss." But I wondered why he believed in something like astrology that, in my perspective, was just another new-age ego reification attachment based in unscientific and unscrupulous myth? Why did he desire other substances to be in his mind so often if his mind was already completely settled and content with how everything is here and now?

The more we talked, I noticed the desire in me growing to understand, to figure it out. For me, that is a very obvious sign of my ego trying to make some things happen. I could see that these questions weren't really about him. They were about me. Did I (mis)understand enlightenment? Had the awakening that I had experienced to ultimate reality been full "enlightenment," or were there other stages of spiritual development that I had yet to attain? Did any of that categorization really matter?

The ego can be a clever bastard sometimes. In this case, my ego had tried to move from the experience of freedom to an identity of freedom. It was similar, even if far more subtle, than the old internal struggles of whether to believe or not believe in God, how to control my music career, or come to peace with Lucie's Down syndrome diagnosis. It was a snag, like a tiny, invisible edge of a fingernail catching on silk. It was another toy in some corner of my mind wanting to be a real boy, a shadow that wanted to be a special *someone* who was enlightened. But alas, toys cannot be boys, and illusory, grasping egos can't be enlightened any more than closing fists can be opening hands.

That snag became yet another attachment that had to be let go of repeatedly before I eventually felt the constriction fully release. When it finally did, it literally felt like a tiny and subtle knot being uncoiled in my brain. That shadowy sense of self that had reemerged from the depths of my mind with its desire to be an enlightened self simply disappeared into the night, and there was, once again, just *THIS*.

When the river reveals these sorts of shadows and unearthed constrictions in us, it is a great grace. One must first realize that some part of their body/mind is holding onto something in order to let it go. Letting go: That's the one spiritual move (or unmove). It's not even something that you "do" as much as something you stop doing. It's not belief as much as it's trust. It's not trying to change anything, but simply being.

We cannot choose to do this or that *in order* to someday attain enlightenment. Such an act would still be an act of grasping. *Trying* to let go is still clinging. Letting go *is* enlightenment.

Of course, there may be times your body just isn't ready to let go. The karma simply hasn't run itself out yet. The trauma has not been worked out of your muscles in a safe space yet. And that's okay. In the same way that I can't drop a pencil and honestly expect it to float in midair, I can't force my mind or body to let go of things that they aren't ready to let go of, because there isn't a separate *self* within my body to control my body with.

A separate *I* is an illusion, a story being told in my brain. In fact, recent brain studies have shown that the prefrontal cortex—the part of the brain implicated in much of our personality, planning, and overall captaining of the ship—seems to be sort of like a storyteller that is often just watching things happen in other parts of the brain and then telling the story within the conscious experience that "I did that." You can directly observe the "I'm making this happen" phenomenon by simply observing your breath for a while. You can make it seem like "you" are consciously controlling your breath, but, of course, when you stop doing that, your breath continues perfectly naturally without a break between conscious and unconscious "control." In reality, there is no real, separate *you* controlling anything. By the time you consciously decide to do something, brain scans have shown that other parts of the brain had already started things in motion. The narrator of your consciousness just catches up a split second later with its "decision."

This can be either a freeing or frustrating realization. Most of us are clutching the bar on the roller coaster, hoping to in some way control the ride. Others of us throw our hands in the air and laugh through the screams. Regardless of the illusory nature of the free will of the ego, we do all have experience, at least, of the subjective reality of making decisions; so, practically speaking, if there is anything to *do* with these ego snags, shadows, and constrictions that come up within us, it's just to notice the tension and then let it go as much and as often as you feel able to. While sheer effort cannot make you something you are not (you're already *THIS*), the subjective experience of effort is necessary for you to meditate, to practice, to go to therapy, to do whatever it is that you need to do in order to see what you feel like you need to see and let go of what you need to let go of.

Be kind and patient with yourself in this process of becoming free. To worry about it does nothing except exacerbate the problem. We cannot practice spirituality in order to discover freedom; the practice of spirituality *is* freedom. The time, energy, and practice is simply the training of our bodies and minds to not continue to grasp at the futility of our illusions and desires. Freedom is not something to be found somewhere else, it is simply *THIS*—here and now. There is *nothing* to be attained. No self to improve. Nothing to practice and no one to do the practicing. There is no battle to be won. There is nothing to lose and nothing to gain. Enlightenment is simply the most *natural* way for a human to be (even if that sometimes means a bit of weed or astrology are involved).

Putting *THIS* into practice is the simple and natural surrender to the infinite and eternal creative life of the ever-unfolding now. It is "Not my will, but Thine be done." Or as Ram Dass might say, just watch it all happening here and now, baby.

How a specific wave reaches the shore is not up to any individual wave. But when I stop spending all my mental energy on the futility that is resisting the current, I am free—not free in the sense that I, little ego me, can do whatever I want or that I never experience loss, pain, or sadness, but free in the sense that there is nothing to be afraid of anymore. All of these emotions are simply happenings—another movement of the water, another timbre within the symphony. When you see *THIS*, you are free to fully experience it all, unfettered and wildly alive.

Practicing Being

> *"Draw bamboos for ten years, become a bamboo, then forget all about bamboos when you are drawing."* —GEORGE DUTHUIT

I n the last chapter we saw that freedom is letting go. Salvation is surrender. Knowing this, we can see that we need not practice meditation in order to try to get closer to enlightenment. Meditation is enlightenment.

Early in the spiritual path, many of us tend to think of spirituality as some sort of austere *other* to ordinary life. But like Brother Lawrence, a seventeenth-century monk who famously "practiced the presence of God" primarily by washing dishes in his monastery, we can learn to "pray without ceasing." I used to think that Paul's admonition to pray without ceasing meant that I had to figure out how to think about something else (God) while doing ordinary things. But that's not what freedom is. It's actually the opposite. Freedom is not getting pulled away from *THIS* into *that*. Brother Lawrence did not need to work to try to abstract God into language and think about *that* while washing those dishes. On the contrary, the more fully present he was with those dishes, the more fully present he was with God.

When spiritual practice is about somewhere other than here or now, it is not good spiritual practice. That is nothing but ego gratification. Good spiritual practice is whatever helps us become more present to *THIS*. With that in mind, it is clear to me that most of the heavy lifting in my spiritual practice has been done with music.

Music is something that is always and only experienced in a present moment. You can notate representations of sounds in a way that will lead a skilled musician to play music in a particular sequence, rhythm, and emphasis. You can discuss the harmonic theory that the composer had in mind. You can try to extract meaning from and describe past performances of music, or analyze the planned instrumentation choices or song structure, but you can't ever experience music itself except within the precision of a moment. As a musician, to hesitate is to miss the beat, to lose your place. On the other hand, to rush—to get too anxious or excited and then to force something to occur before its time—is awkward to the ear. To play *musically*, one must become, as the Zen Buddhists might say, like a ball floating on the river. The note must be played not too early and not too late but simply where it ought to be. The most musically mature people are those who have learned to relax and let the music happen through them. Good music is never a result of forceful competition between performers trying to overpower one another but of people finding a common flow with one another. With music, there is only flowing with it or not flowing with it. In fact, the music *is* the flow. But getting there takes practice.

There have been a few times after a musical performance that I have been asked about the scales I was using while improvising. Those asking this question have often been aspiring improvisers themselves who want to take something concrete from the performance that they can practice at home. Mastering new scales is, after all, a necessary discipline for any competent improviser. Unfortunately, I never have a very practical answer to give these curious concertgoers because I don't think of scales anymore while I am improvising on a stage. In fact, I'm rarely thinking of anything at all during a performance, especially if it's a good one. In those moments, my mind and body have simply melded into the music. The notes I play are more like breathing than thinking. If there's any thought, it's the sound of the music itself, and not the theoretical building blocks like scales that make it up. Of course, to get to this point, I had to do a hell of a lot of thinking about scales.

When one first begins to learn to improvise, it is not usually best to immediately dive into the deep end of the pool of free jazz or avant-garde composition, but instead to start with something simple. For instance, the teacher may play something like a C7 chord, and the student is instructed to spontaneously play some sort of melody over the top of the chord. But of the infinite possibilities before the student, how is she supposed to know what to play without it sounding like utter nonsense? This is where scales become helpful. Scales provide the basis for the idea of "correct" notes. If the chord is a C7, the teacher will teach a series of notes (a mixolydian scale, for example) that will sound generally pleasing to the ear within that C7 context. C notes, the student learns, are correct. C# notes are not correct. The student is instructed to go home and practice that C mixolydian scale over and over again until it is clean, comfortable, and internalized. The mastery of this scale will eventually allow the aspiring improviser to freely play any of the notes in the scale without worrying that any of them are going to ring out as dissonant or unpleasing to the ear. By knowing the scale, she does not necessarily need to know what every note she plays is going to sound like before she plays it in order for her to improvise a relatively "correct" solo. She can simply trust the scale to not lead her astray.

As time goes on, and the improviser becomes more confident with that C mixolydian scale, perhaps she learns a new scale that can be used over a C7 chord—a G minor pentatonic scale, for example. By playing only the notes in a G minor pentatonic scale, the improviser can elicit a different sort of feeling over the exact same chord. At this stage, she still doesn't need to know exactly what every note will sound like before she plays it, but as she becomes more acquainted with the feelings of the two different "correct" scales, she can alternate between them in order to elicit the general feelings of those scales as she desires.

As the improviser continues to practice and grow through the years, she will likely add many other scales to her toolbox, each with their own unique flavor. At a certain point of her musical development, something interesting begins to happen; she begins to internalize the sound and feeling of the scales in the same way that one internalizes the rules of grammar or the natural cadence of a native language. At some point, all of the scales and feelings of those scales become like second nature, and she no longer needs to think in terms of scales during an improvisational performance any more than she needs to think in terms of the alphabet while having a conversation with someone. At some point, the guard rails fall off, and there is just the sound of the notes played over the chord. At this point, there are no more "correct" notes, no more rules or guidelines or structures of limitation. There is only the music, only *THIS*.

Isn't this also how it goes with religion? When we are young, we need someone to tell us the appropriate places to place our fingers on the frets. Thou shalt not steal. Thou shalt not kill. Thou shalt not commit adultery. Love thy neighbor as thyself. For years, we need to practice those scales, trying to learn how to not be completely selfish ass-holes all of the time. We learn how to love. Eventually, after years and decades of diligent practice, we start shedding the training wheels. We don't need the Ten Commandments posted on our wall in order to not steal. We just don't want to steal. Early on in our spiritual practice, we need black-and-white rules that tell us what is permissible and what is not. Eventually, as we mature, we are able to handle more complexity and nuance. We are able to see that there is no such thing as an "incorrect note" or that "everything is permissible, but not everything is beneficial."

The sort of maturity required to skillfully navigate the gray spaces usually takes many years of disciplined, hard work. Handing a trumpet to someone who doesn't play and saying, "there are no wrong notes," will not result in the same sort of music that came from the lips of genre-defying Miles Davis. One must learn to walk before learning to run. You can't effectively break the rules until you know the rules. I think this is where mystics come from.

As I have learned more about the different mystical traditions in the world, it has struck me how the great traditions all start sounding the same at a certain depth. At the outer (exoteric) and shallower (fundamentalist) levels of religion, every tradition is incredibly different—some wear robes and bells and chant om to themselves, while others wear skinny jeans and put on rock-and-roll shows on Sunday mornings for a bearded being in the sky. But when you find the people who have seriously practiced their scales for decades—those who have lost their own ego supremacy in the nondual fullness of *THIS*—they all start sounding a lot alike. For example, the teachings and spirituality of Father Richard Rohr (a Christian, Franciscan mystic) have a lot more in common with Ram Dass (a Hindu mystic), Hafiz (a Sufi mystic), or even Lao-Tzu (credited as the founder of Taoism) than they do with most other Christian teachings you might come across. I think this is because when you hear a master play, you are not simply hearing the fearful steps of a person trying to remain within an individual scale anymore. At this stage of spiritual maturity, there are no more "wrong notes." A person like Richard Rohr is not afraid of traditions or metaphors outside his own. In fact, he's learned from them.

Improvisers have personalities. They have likes and dislikes, and some masterful improvisers that have transcended individual scales still tend to sound more at home in some scales than in others. Father Rohr talks about Christ a lot. Ram Dass talks about Maharaj-ji a lot. But neither of them are trapped inside of their own stories. The individual scales have been transcended to the place where there is only the music—only *THIS*.

The reason music and religion have been my primary spiritual practices is not because music and religion are superior to other human disciplines, but because these are the primary stories I've inhabited in my life. The truths of *THIS* could just as easily be spoken of through the lens and language of business, law, science, fashion, sports, food, or any other story that people experience *THIS* through.

THIS doesn't happen somewhere other than your normal, boring, everyday life. Nirvana is not limited to meditation retreats or sensory-deprivation float tanks. It is also a way of experiencing staff meetings and rush-hour traffic. Freedom from suffering doesn't necessarily mean you get a new job or a bunch more free time to bliss out on acid. Freedom is being in on the Joke and playing it however you'd like. It is watching your boss get mad at you with the underlying confidence that it's just a dream. When you know you're dreaming, you're free to play whatever games you wish.

Letting go is freedom, but it is not simply freedom to dissipate into oneness. It is freedom to *be*. And to be human means to create, to tell and embody stories.

As I explored in my first book, *The Crowd, the Critic, and the Muse: A Book for Creators*,[21] to be a human being is to be a creator. It is to imagine a world and then shape the world around one into that image. This way of being and making is not limited to the fine arts, but to all human endeavor. Accountants use spreadsheets; painters use canvases; carpenters, hammers and saws—but all rearrange reality according to their perceptions and desires. We are made of stories, and those stories are inherently generative. We are music making music. We are spotlights, wandering through infinity, shining our awareness here and there, discovering and creating order with our imaginations.

But as we've seen, the cost of being this sort of being is that *life is suffering*. We get caught in our own stories like

21. Michael Gungor, *The Crowd, The Critic, and the Muse: A Book for Creators* (Denver: Woodsley Press, 2012).

an actor forgetting he is playing a part, and we take the
weight of the world onto our shoulders. Freedom from
that has been the entire point of this book. So how and
why would one create anything in the world from a place
of nondual awareness where everything is already experienced as music? How does one judge one particular lyric
to be "better" than another if he knows that all words
are already the perfect lyrical expression of *THIS*? How
does one decide which story to tell in her film if all stories
go together and are all seen as exquisite, interconnected
constructs of the mind and equally beautiful expressions
of the ineffable? How does one change the world through
activism if one does not fundamentally desire for *THIS* to
be anything other than it is? Isn't clinging to that desire for
the world to be other than it is the very root of suffering
that we've been examining for this entire book until now?

Yes. But—pay attention to the subtlety here—the way that
the world is also includes your desire to change the world.

Think of a bird that builds her nest. Is a bird's nest
really the product of that one particular bird desiring
the world to be other than it is? Or are the instincts with
which she builds the nest part of the way the world is? Isn't
any single bird's nest really a creation of all birdkind and
not simply a separate bird ego? And beyond that, isn't all
birdkind really a creation of the entire ecosystem of Earth?
Keep zooming back far enough, and eventually there is no
bird making anything. There is only *THIS* telling stories.

So how do we create the world anew when we see that
it's all already perfect? Perhaps we can answer this question
with another question: How does the sun decide what sort
of light to shine?

The sun doesn't decide what sort of light to shine. It is
the sun. The sun shines. The sun is its shining. In the same
way, you are not simply your body, but you are also what
your body does. There is no separate *you* who breathes. You
are the breath as much as the breather and the breathing.

In the same way, there is no *you* who creates or imagines. You are that creation and imagination.

As I write this book, I have to choose which words to write. To do that, I have to have a desire of some kind that interacts with a mythic framework of some kind, but that doesn't mean that the brain with these desires and mythic framework needs to create some feedback loop within itself that thinks of itself as an "I" that has to "decide" between this possibility or that one. When this happens, it just stalls the engine. It is possible to create in a way where one does not stall, but instead spontaneously and naturally creates just as the sun spontaneously and naturally shines.

When I used to go into the studio to record a song, I had all of these stories that my ego wanted to try to create of its own accord. I (the little, illusory I) was to be the creator, and so I had a list of questions and stories that I felt needed to be seriously addressed:

> *Was this song clever enough?*
> *Was it hip/fresh/unique enough?*
> *Was I making a difference in the world with this music?*
> *Was I being true to myself?*

On and on, the stories looped onto each other. And truth is, anytime I would start thinking like that, it would lock me up. The creative engine would stall. It was only when something directly caught my full attention that I was able to move forward into creating. A chord would draw me in. An instrumentation choice would present itself and the illusion of choice would disappear. That instrumentation simply was what would be in the song. There was no other choice to make.

To *try* to create is to stall the creative engine that is your mind and body. Children do not *try* to play. They simply play. In the same way, you do not need to try to imagine, innovate, create, or change the world. You simply can be what you already are—a human being with an imagination and desires to create and change the world. Again, the difference between spiritual freedom and spiritual captivity is not that in freedom you lose all of your uniqueness, emotions, and desires. Freedom is when you are no longer imprisoned by *clinging* to those stories.

When we cling to our desires, beliefs, aesthetic preferences, personality traits, or any other stories, we actually limit our ability to freely be who we are at any given moment. We doubt ourselves. We hesitate. We stall the engine.

In *Zen and the Art of Archery*,[22] Eugen Herrigel describes how it took him years of training with a Zen master to be able to release the string of his bow without *intending* to do it. Day after day, he would pull back the string of the large Japanese bow, and try to bring it to its absolute farthest point of tension before letting go as he had been instructed. But every time he did this, the arrow would jerk a little upon its release. Even though the master demonstrated a perfectly smooth shot time after time, the student couldn't get the hang of it. The master told him to not try to intentionally release the string, but just to let it happen naturally and automatically, like a ripened fruit falling from a tree. Month after month, year after year, Herrigel failed to understand what his teacher meant.

In his third year of study, the student took some time during a break between lessons and figured out how to manipulate the muscles in his hand to simulate the natural, smooth shot. It was not the same effortless action as the teacher had instructed him with, but he found that it did the job—the arrow flew straight. When he arrived back with his master, he was instructed to shoot. He did. He contorted his muscles with effort, but the shot looked perfect. It soared smoothly and reached its intended target. The teacher looked at him blankly. He instructed him to shoot again. The result of the second shot was even better, technically speaking, than the first. The master said nothing. He

22. Eugen Herrigel, *Zen in the Art of Archery* (New York: Pantheon, 1953).

simply snatched the bow away from Herrigel and went to his cushion, sitting with his back to his cheating pupil.

Herrigel had to beg the teacher to resume lessons with him, but the teacher made it clear that he would only continue if Herrigel promised to never try to cheat the art again. After all, for the Japanese, archery isn't just a sport like it is for us Westerners. For them, like swordsmanship, flower arranging, or tea ceremonies, it's not only an art but a spiritual practice. I recently met a woman who was in her seventh year of studying to be a "tea master." She told me that it usually takes at least twelve years, and after seven, she still didn't know if she would have what it takes. To serve tea. . . . Very different mind-set than we have in America.

After Herrigel promised to not cheat again, he said it was like he was starting over; his years of practice felt wasted. He continued to ask for clarification on how he could possibly shoot the arrow without being the one to shoot it. The teacher would tell him to stop thinking and just let *it* shoot.

Herrigel would complain that it was impossible and that the tension just gets too painful.

"You only feel it because you haven't really let go of yourself. It's all so simple. You can learn from an ordinary bamboo leaf what ought to happen. It bends lower and lower under the weight of snow. Suddenly, the snow slips to the ground without the leaf having stirred."

One day, after firing an arrow that missed the target entirely, the master turned and bowed to Herrigel, telling him that this was a right shot. Upon hearing this, the pupil was excited. The teacher cautioned him to not take it as a compliment. It had nothing to do with him. He just hadn't gotten in the way of that one and *it* had shot, rather than his clamoring ego. Eventually, Herrigel learned how to shoot without shooting. The target merged with the archer, the pulling with the pulled, the releasing with the released.

The mind-set that we live, create, and work from is not

something we often pay as much attention to in the capital-
istic and colonial-minded West. We are often so focused on
productivity, efficiency, and deadlines that we lose touch with
the nuances of the work and any reverence for the process of
what we are doing. In this way, we step out of the flow of nature and into that old myth of separateness that results in us
plundering and conquering the world rather than harmoniz-
ing and flowing within it. There are no big award ceremonies
like the Grammys or Oscars for Zen tea masters or archers.
A master in these disciplines doesn't do it to show off or
receive glory. They do it as the one-pointed action of their
being. The sun shines. Birds make nests. Humans drink tea.

I think we would do well in the age of Kardashians
and viral videos to learn from this ancient wisdom. Many
of us are just constantly scattering our half-baked creative
projects to the wind as quickly as possible, hoping that
someone notices and subscribes. Many of us have lost the
art of good, patient, invisible work, and end up missing out
on some of the great joys of quietly, diligently honing our
craft (not to mention what all of the shitty, lowest-common-
denominator "viral" work is doing to our collective
spirituality, work ethic, and sense of aesthetics as a society).

I think the artist, writer, painter, archer, teacher, busi-
nessperson, and all the rest of us who imagine worlds into
being would do well to pay more attention to not only what
we are creating but to the stories that we are creating from.
The fruit of the tree, after all, is tied to the deepest roots
of the tree. We often focus on getting enough fruit in the
basket, even when we've forgotten to water the roots.

For me, this is how all of this gets put into practice:
When I go into my studio or writing space to work, I try
to first pay attention to my body. Before I just jump into
crafting the world, I make sure I'm in a useful emotional,
spiritual, and mental state to cooperate with the flow of the
stories I want to be inhabiting. Do I want to embody stories
of fear, separateness, and violence, or of love, connectedness,

and peace? I then do whatever I need to in order to get into the state of "faith" (described as the substance of things hoped for by the author of the book of Hebrews) that these particular stories require, and then I simply show up and lay back into the flow of the river. When I am fully present in *THIS*, I am able to work for the joy of the present moment rather than rushing toward my imagined end goal. By this, I don't mean the same thing as the sort of visionless, "present moment" approach to work employed by so much haphazard YouTube, music, or podcast content seeking trendiness with no thought to its lasting value. I'm certainly not saying "just light some incense and have a good creative philosophy, and you'll be able to write your masterpiece." Good work takes discipline, practice, time, patience, and vision. The creator still has the responsibility of refining the craft. To get the blisters on her fingers after shredding scales all day or the sore neck after the long hours at his writing desk. But it is possible to engage in the hard task of working without the burden of getting in the work's way. It is possible to let go in a way that you become like moldable clay in the hands of a skilled potter rather than trying to make your ego be potter, clay, and wheel.

While creating good work does often necessitate imagining something other than here and now, that imagination always exists only here and now. When even our planning and patience is rooted in the contentment of *THIS*, we can slow down enough to not only create better work but to enjoy the process. When we allow love to be the context and setting for *THIS* to occur within, we are free to follow the natural desires of our hearts to imagine and create new worlds. Here, after the noisy ego feedback loops have been silenced and the hard work of practice has been done, all that is left is to let the bow shoot its arrow, to simply enjoy the music of the moment that is happening like a child playing with dolls. This dab of paint. This sixteenth note. This period at the end of this sentence.

Telling Good Stories

T he direct, fully awake experience of *THIS* isn't imprisoned within myth or story. Here, the sensuous universe of taking a sip of cool water is not mistaken with concepts like "sip," "cool," or "water." *THIS* is beyond words, category, or distinction. It simply and fully is. Still, the stories we inhabit provide a context and setting for *THIS* to be experienced within for both ourselves and others. Whether we create war or peace, life or death, love or hate, all depends on the stories that we experience *THIS* through.

Some stories enliven and create new worlds while others imprison, oppress, and destroy worlds. Some offer the possibility of a meaningful, enriched life; others offer only a cold, dead nihilism. So what sorts of stories are worth telling and creating the world from? That seems to me to be one of the most important questions we could ask.

If one could imagine stories being like trees, some of the stories, like Christianity, Hinduism, Judaism, Islam, or Buddhism, are like ancient and towering redwoods. In their branches are entire ecosystems of life—sects and denominations that span the globe over millennia. These elders of the forest have sheltered and sustained life for generations, offering frameworks for people to find identity, community, safety, purpose, and meaning within. And even if we don't fully embrace their teachings, I think each deserves our respect. There are other plants in this forest that are younger and perhaps less majestic sometimes—myths like capitalism, democracy, constructs of race, political party, or scientific materialism. Any of these plants may grow into towering trees someday, too, but time has not yet made clear what the long-term effects of these stories will be, how much life can be sustained within them, or whether or not their stalks and trunks are healthy and sturdy enough to grow tall.

While I no longer identify exclusively with any one of these trees, I do have great respect and reverence for the unique wisdom that I feel each of them offers. In the following three chapters, I'd like to tell three stories about the nature of *THIS* that I have discovered as I have walked through the forest. The three stories are:

THIS is God.
THIS is Awareness.
THIS is Love.

Each of these three stories is an attempt at a sort of harmonization between what are normally considered to be contradictory stories. As someone who has done a bit of swinging from tree to tree, I have noticed some common threads and harmonies between the big traditions and the newer stories that sometimes get overlooked by people who prefer sitting in just one tree. Here, I hope to relay these stories in a way that can not only enrich our own lives and work, but also help us find common ground with those whose metaphors differ from our own.

Humanity often divides itself into groups of "us" versus "them," resulting in incredible suffering, violence, and fear. For the sake of the one human organism, it seems to me that finding ways of seeking a harmony between paradoxes (East and West, mystical and scientific, theistic and nontheistic . . . etc.) is a worthwhile endeavor.

My hope is that you find ways in which these tales can not only serve you and deepen your felt experience and derived meaning of *THIS* but can also help you live out your ever-unfolding freedom in ways that love and serve others. Of course, I hope that you will keep in mind what we've explored up to this point—that stories easily become prisons if you take them too seriously. Canvas can provide a home for magnificent art, but an artist can't get too attached to the look of their naked canvas, or they may forget to ruin it with paint. When we cling to the stories on which we color our worlds too tightly, we trade *THIS* for *that*; we confuse background for foreground, music theory for music itself. So I invite you to explore these meaning-making stories with me with an open heart and a playful spirit, lest, God forbid, you fall into the trap of *believing* a single word of them.

THIS Is God

"Whoever knows himself knows God."—MUHAMMAD

W hy, after everything that I've experienced in my travels in Christianity, atheism, etc., would I want to bring the G word back into this? Is there any word so charged, so polarizing? Any single word that is responsible for more bloodshed, more fear, more shame, more oppression or repression?

From the Crusades to Manifest Destiny to slavery to present-day arguments against evolution or gay marriage, God has so often been used on the wrong side of history to justify injustice, sloppy thinking, and unspeakable cruelty.

It may sound harsh to cut off her clitoris, but it's Allah's will, as revealed in the Koran. . . .

Why even bother with such an abused, loaded, and ambiguously defined word? If people kept killing people over the word "bing-bong," but nobody even could agree on what "bing-bong" meant, wouldn't it be better to just come up with some new language rather than spending more energy on debating whether Jesus Christ was really the only begotten bing-bong or whether or not bing-bong could hear our prayers?

Our attachment to the word *God* is bizarre when you think about it. It's as if the latest Gallup poll shows that 90 percent of Americans believe in bing-bongs, but zero percent of them know what the fuck a bing-bong even is! There are schools that give out doctorate degrees to people for becoming bing-bong experts, and there are entire book industries that sell millions of books that both prove and disprove the existence of bing-bongs. And frankly, this is why I'm still talking about God. Because, we humans are really obsessed with that word. Despite the best attempts of the New Atheists, the word *God* isn't going anywhere anytime soon. So, I figure that if we are all going to be pledging allegiance and singing anthems to bing-bongs anyway, we might as well at least tell better stories about them than the ones responsible for genocides and Christian rock.

It's not just that, though. What other word can we use for the ultimate reality underneath it all in which we live and move and have our being? What other word so quickly gets to the core of our felt assumptions and wranglings about the meaning of life, the nature of being, or the destiny of humankind? We can use words like *THIS*, *Source*, *All*, or *Ground of Being* as often as we like, but those words will never resonate so loudly in this culture or in my own ears, frankly, as *God* does. That's the English version of the word we as a Western civilization have chosen. It's the word I grew up with. It's the word printed on our money and prayed to at our gravesides, and we all already have our assumptions about what the word means. *God* is not ignorable or erasable, so we might as well think carefully about how we think of it.

So, setting aside the question of whether God exists or not for a moment, who or what should we even think of when someone uses the word *God*?

Good luck on finding a single, agreeable answer on that question. Even within the Bible of a single religion, you find a God who both commands people to love their enemies[23] and for his people to commit genocide.[24] Even with the same author (Paul) within the same New Testament of the same Bible, you can find both a view of God with whom "there is no more male or female"[25] and a view of a God who wants women to cover their heads,[26] to remain silent in the church,[27] and not have authority over a man because it was Eve who was deceived, not Adam.[28] Still, as varied as the theological views of God may be within Christianity

23. Matthew 5:44. 26. 1 Corinthians 11:6.
24. Deuteronomy 7. 27. 1 Corinthians 14:34.
25. Galatians 3:28. 28. 1 Timothy.

and in the Bible itself—whether God is the angry bearded guy in the sky or the loving All in All in which we live and move and have our being—most Christians would agree that God is the one who created the universe (even if that was by means of evolution through natural selection) and the one who raised Jesus from the dead. But this is not how other religions would think of God, obviously.

Some of the other great religions of the world from the East, such as Hinduism, Buddhism, and Taoism, have a very different concept of ultimate reality (God) than the Christian one. In these stories, God is not someone who stands apart from his creation like a potter and a pot. Instead, God (Brahman, the Tao, the Void, etc.) is seen as the fundamental and ultimate reality or *self* that gives rise to and as everything that is. From this perspective, we are God grown from God in a way that has led us to forget who we really are. There is no fundamental divide between creation and its creator here, only the illusion of it.

In the monotheistic religions like Judaism, Islam, and Christianity, saying "I am God" is at the top of the heresy list. Saying that sort of thing has been known to get folks in trouble—burned-alive and nailed-to-crosses levels of trouble. Why? Maybe because in the Christian understanding of God, a statement like "I am God" either is a statement of an unfathomably delusional ego or someone who does not identify with their ego, and either way, that person is dangerous. In fact, the latter is probably even more dangerous because a person who doesn't primarily identify with their ego isn't likely to put a lot of stock in the earthly ruling powers that be.

"Bow before me!" says the empire! If you're a reasonable ego, you tremble and bow. If you're God, you're free to laugh at yourself.

Human empire is, after all, built on myths of authority and hierarchy and power—all silliness when one realizes that all of the suns in the universe are burning within your own heart. This is why saying "I am God" is perhaps the highest heresy in so much religious empire. If you are God, then who can we manipulate with shame and sexual mores to fall in line and cough up the cash?

There have certainly been Christian mystics like St. Francis of Assisi, Julian of Norwich, St. John of the Cross, St. Teresa of Ávila, Pseudo-Dionysius the Areopagite, and many others who have experienced and recounted a more seamless reality between creation and creator than most Christian thought is willing to allow. And, of course, there is Jesus who was a Jew, not a Christian, but is the one for whom Christianity is named, very clearly claiming unity with God. There are also a few verses here and there—"In Him we live and move and have our being"[29] or "From him, through him, and to him are all things"[30] or that "Christ is all and in all"[31]—that might hint at a more mystical union between the divine and material reality. Still, on average, Christianity would teach that God is somehow fundamentally separate from his creation. God is thought of as a single divine being in three persons, Father, Son, and Holy Spirit, who created the universe by his word like a potter forming his clay.

In most Christian theology, human sin deepens the fundamental divide between God and his creation in a way that can only be bridged or restored through Jesus, the only begotten Son of God. Through Jesus, God can dwell within us, and through faith in Christ, we can dwell with God for all of eternity. Still, even in the restoration of the relationship between God and humankind through Jesus, the Christian imagination usually maintains a strict fundamental boundary between the creator and the created. We may be invited into communion with God for eternity, but not into full union with God as God. Other "monotheistic" religions like Judaism and Islam often have similar outlooks on the gulf between God and his creation, even if the specific doctrines and stories that describe how this divide is healed vary.

29. Acts of the Apostles 17:28.
30. Romans 11:36.
31. Colossians 3:11.

In the ancient Indian and Chinese philosophies, there is no real divide between God and humans. In these stories, our sense of aloneness and alienation from our source is because we (God) are lost in our own games of make-believe and magic.

Even for post-Christians in the West who may not be particularly concerned about heresy, saying "I am God" sounds egotistical and absurd. But this is because we are hearing it through our myths that assume the ego to be a real and separate *thing* from its source. In this Christian or post-Christian mythic context, saying "I am God" feels like stretching out our ego to the size of infinity because in this myth, there is no possible conception beyond the patchwork, fractured framework in which the ego is the fundamentally real, supreme, and unquestioned reality of the universe ("I think, therefore I am").

In other mythic contexts, like Hinduism, saying "I am God" is a realization born from letting go of the false ego stories that make one feel like a someone who could be separate from God.

Christianity sees this view of God and shakes its sternly frowned countenance—"that's *pantheism!*"

I remember when I first came across the idea of pantheism in my Christian school as a kid, and we laughed at how those primitive people on the other side of the world thought that a tree or a rock was God. Why would you worship a tree or a rock rather than the God who created them? What we failed to see was all of the cosmological and metaphysical assumptions we were making in that question, which elevated our own egos to the position of ultimate reality. More on that in a moment. First, it's worth noting that *pantheism* is not native to Buddhism, Hinduism, or Taoism. It is a word Western Christians (mis)used to categorize a conception of God in all and as all. It is a bit of a misguided caricature though because it still carries with it the inherent assumption of fundamental separateness and ego supremacy of Christendom. This would be a little like defining *Star Wars* plot points with *Star Trek* terms. They are different mythic universes. Saying that Luke "beamed up" his light saber is not quite right.

In these so-called "pantheistic" myths from places like India, China, and Japan, the universe is not thought of in the same way as it is in the empires built from European Christendom. In the Christian imagination, the universe is usually felt to be a set of fundamentally separate things and events. In the Hindu imagination, God is not simply the sum of a bunch of separate things, as the Christian term "pantheism" infers. Nor would they claim that a rock or tree as a separate thing or event has the power to (in and by itself) create or sustain a universe. *Pantheism*, then, is a word used on the outside of the Eastern stories and rarely by one who understands those perspectives.

Today, as I survey the ancient "tree" stories and how different the universes are in their tellings, I find value in both the Christian and Hindu imagination. The assumed separateness at the core of Christianity has, for example, amplified the worth of the individual in ways that certain aspects of Indian culture, like the caste system, have not. Christian cosmology and theology have made room for ideas like equality, social justice, body autonomy, and the pursuit of individual happiness in ways that are more difficult to imagine from the perspective of the beggar and the prince being essentially one and the same Godhead.

Still, every good thing has its limits, and I have found that there is a cost to the egocentrism inherent in Christianity, and a truth, wisdom, and beauty in the stories of Hinduism, Buddhism, and Taoism that are missing from the traditional Christian imagination almost entirely.

To a Christian, the idea that Christianity is inherently egocentric might be a foreign or disagreeable concept. Christianity is supposed to be about Jesus, right? We learned in Christian school that our faith was not about ourselves

but about God and "his story" (history . . . wah wah wah—
that's that edgy Christian-school humor). But I would like
to suggest that all of Christianity's it's-not-about-me talk is
actually a very clever way for egos to reign as the supreme
reality in the Christian myth.

Let's go back to the Bible again. Before Copernicus
came along in the sixteenth century, claiming heretically
that the earth revolved around the sun, everybody[32] thought
that Earth was literally the center of the universe. This
view of reality where a tiny, young (approximately six
thousand years old, according to the biblical genealogies)
universe literally revolved around the human ego was the
cosmological viewpoint that the Bible was written out of.
There are over two hundred verses that refer to the world
as being some sort of unmoving object with a dome spread
out above it. Isaiah speaks of God being "enthroned above
the circle of the earth." In Daniel 4, there is a tree that
grew so high that one could see it "to the end of all the
earth." The entire Bible envisions the universe as a three-
tiered reality where the earth is a flat, stationary disk at the
center of the cosmos, above which there is a "firmament"
that separated the heavens from the earth, and below which
is Sheol, the place of the dead. Even God took his proper
place on the stage of this human-centered universe by
making his home "up there" in the heavens.

In the creation narrative of Genesis, God takes five days
to set the stage by creating the rest of the universe before
he finally gets to the grand finale of the sixth day when he
makes his masterpiece, his pièce de résistance, his magnum
opus, the crown jewel of his creation that is to be crafted in
his very own perfect image—*meeeeeee*, the human ego.

*"But how could we say that the human ego is the center of every-
thing if human beings are such a fragile and short-lived phenomenon
within the universe?"* the skeptic may ask.

Humans are only short-lived because the human ego
made a mistake! (Says the story.)

32. Other than, perhaps, a few notable exceptions like Aristarchus of Sa-
mos, who unsuccessfully presented a similar cosmological model eighteen
centuries earlier.

All evil, suffering, entropy, and death in the entire universe is because of a single ego's sin. That's how powerful the ego is! Adam, following his *female* partner's lead, ate the fruit of a forbidden tree, and this caused a rift to happen within the universe between heaven and earth, which paved the way for all of this evil that we see around us.

"Wait a minute," the skeptic says, incredulously. *"Are you saying that the reason that asteroids struck the earth, creating ice ages that killed off billions of living organisms millions of years before the first human would walk the earth was because a naked lady in a garden ate the wrong piece of fruit? Are you really saying that none of the trillions of planets in our universe have ever had life on them except our planet? Or if those planets have had or currently have life on them, are you really saying that the reason those life forms die, or feel pain in childbirth, or get cancer, or anything like that is all because of the sinful hearts within one of the species of ape on a tiny 'pale blue dot' in the Milky Way galaxy?"*

Yes. Whether or not that sin was seen as a literal naked woman eating fruit from the wrong tree because a talking snake tricked her, or whether that story is a metaphor for some sort of primal sinful human condition, the narrative told from Genesis to Revelation to the seven ecumenical councils of the early church to the thoughts of C. S. Lewis to the pews of First Baptist Church of Toledo last Sunday morning is that human sin caused the Fall, and the Fall is responsible for all of the evil in the universe. The Fall is what Jesus came to correct. He came to die to reverse the curse, to bridge the gap, to pay the price, to take our place and heal creation.

I heard a famous preacher give a sermon one time about cosmology, and at the end, he showed a slide of a nebula that looked a little like a cross. Not surprising that he could find one shaped like that, given the fact that there are countless nebulae out there. (There's also a crater on the moon that looks a lot like Mickey Mouse if anybody wants to use that information for religious purposes.) But this preacher made the cross-shaped nebula the pinnacle of his sermon. It showed how the work of the cross was at the heart of God through the entire creation process. When one stops to think about all of the implications of God setting up the entire universe in precisely the right way so that approximately two thousand years after Jesus was crucified, a few Christian egos could feel some sense of satisfaction by looking through a telescope and seeing a nebula that looked sort of like the instrument that the Romans used to crucify God's son with, it really is staggering how far the ego can and does go with its storytelling in order to reify and center itself as the supreme reality of the cosmos.

It's no wonder identifying oneself with God is the highest heresy in Christianity. The real God of Christianity is the human ego. It is far more orthodox and acceptable to the tradition to question the existence of God than to question the existence of an ego that could be separate from God.[33]

I don't think Jesus saw the world through the same egocentric lens that the faith named after him has tended to. He did live in a time of the three-tiered cosmological model of the universe, so he understandably still spoke in ways that hinted at God being "up there": "Thy will be done on earth as it is in heaven. . . ." But he didn't speak of God like others did. He didn't speak of God as some being who was far away or living in a temple who had to be appeased. He spoke in relational and identity terms that were so intimate as to be considered heretical by the religious powers of the day.[34]

By the way, after letting Jesus go as some exclusive "lord and savior" for my eternally extended ego, I was eventually able to, thanks to people like Ram Dass and the wisdom within the mythical structures of the Far East, hear his words anew. For so many years, I held firmly onto the belief that Jesus was the clearest picture of God—that really important thought-idol that lived somewhere *out there*—and I

---

33. While atheism is usually considered a sin in Christianity, doubting the existence of God is not considered a sin, but a simple and common temptation. Many famous and beloved saints of the Church (St. Teresa of Calcutta, St. Teresa of Ávila, John of the Cross, etc.) were known to doubt the existence of God. There is even an important spiritual idea known as "the dark night of the soul," in which heavy doubt purifies the faith of the believer.

thought I needed to *believe* in Jesus in order for my ego to be accepted by God. I was told that I had to believe the right things about this Jesus if I wanted to be in paradise rather than burning forever in hell after I died.

It would be difficult to misunderstand Jesus more than this. What, after all, is more egocentric than our views about the "afterlife"? And I'm not just talking about Christians here. There are billions of people from nearly every tradition who live their entire lives around the idea of an afterlife, doing everything they can to ensure that they and their loved ones go to Heaven, or have a good next birth, or get a bunch of virgins in paradise, or have their own planets to chill out on with all their wives and spirit babies.

I think that most people use the stories of disembodied souls, reincarnation, or an afterlife as a really clever way of reifying the ego—as another way of feeling that "I" am fundamentally separate from *THIS*. Like a wave assuming that it will become a wave again somewhere else in the ocean after it crashes against the shore or a fist assuming that there's some metaphysical *afterfist* up in the clouds where fists go after hands open. For many of us, our ego stories are so substantial, we have extended our stories in our minds as far as they can go—to an infinite existence beyond the grave. And again, maybe there really is some sort of illusory separation from the One that somehow contains my memories and mythical "self" constructs from this life. Maybe the individual "I" story does continue beyond the grave in other stories for a while somehow, before reuniting with Brahman in full. I don't know. I don't personally have any memories of dying before.[35] But even if there were an afterlife, the questions would still remain, what is the ultimate Ground that keeps the souls coming back around? Who keeps the heavenly harps in tune? What could there ever be but the infinite, omnipresent *THIS*?

34. Examples include, "before Abraham was born, I am"; "the Father and I are one"; calling God "Abba," which was an intimate term for father; etc.
35. Some sages and mystics claim that they do. And honestly, this is one of the only reasons that I remain "agnostic" about the afterlife rather than simply dismissing the idea altogether as ego wish-fulfillment.

Because I grew up interpreting Jesus's words through this faulty lens that was based on extending the existence of the small sense of "I" that is the ego through eternity, I never could hear the true wisdom of his gospel. Here was this man who said things like, "when you do this for the least of these, you do it for me." He identified not only with an individual ego but with all of humanity—with the poor, sick, and imprisoned. He identified not only as human but as God. "He is the vine, we are the branches." "Whenever you see me, you see the Father." He sought that "we would be one" as he and his Father are one.

Can you hear these words? I didn't used to be able to. I was like the ground, full of thorns that choked out the truth of the words. I used to think that verses like "I am the Way, the Truth, and the Life. No one comes to the Father but through me," meant that Jesus was some sort of narrow door that kept the riffraff out of Heaven. Now I see that Jesus was not speaking from that place of separation—nobody sees the sun but through its light. It's all one, and Jesus saw it, yet he was still a man with great compassion who walked among the poor and oppressed, bringing healing, forgiveness, and love. He lived in a time of great oppression. His land was under occupation from a brutal foreign empire, yet his advice was, "Look at the birds." People were being crucified. Their lands, homes, and lives snatched away. "Look at the flowers." Their identity attacked and dismissed. "Don't worry about tomorrow." Jesus was free.

But being free didn't mean that he didn't care about the suffering of humanity. Jesus didn't just escape into his meditation cave to live in constant bliss (although he did escape the noise of the world quite often). Jesus wept. He got angry and overturned tables. He chastised religious leaders, calling them hypocrites, vipers, and whitewashed tombs. He taught people that God was most clearly found in the unwanted segments of society and that the Kingdom of God would overturn the evil of the world they found themselves in. But the fight would not be like most thought it should be. It would not be with swords or horses or armies, but in being free like a child. The war against oppression would be fought by loving their enemies and blessing those who persecuted them.

Somehow Christendom turned Jesus into an idol to be possessed by the ego as a key for the ego's eternal enduring, rather than the living invitation to fully experience the eternal *THIS*. Christian empires turned the idea of incarnation (God made flesh) into a dead and sterile dogma of exclusivity rather than a lived reality of love. The ruling entities and those leading the developments of Christianity and the Church made Jesus's words more about what will happen in some imagined future after death rather than the eternal life that he pointed to here and now. Growing up, Jesus was presented to me like some sort of superhero who had gone away but would someday come back and make everything better. Jesus was to be found not in the present grittiness of life, like he said he would be,[36] but instead in the traditions of old men and dusty books. We looked for him in the past and the future, when all along he had pointed us to the infinite and eternal present of birds and flowers and neighbors. We keep going back to the places where we thought he was in our belief systems, traditions, and stories of some imagined future, but unless our thoughts, words, and practices ground us in *THIS* very moment, our religion is nothing but an empty tomb, and "he is not here."

As Jesus demonstrated, a life that is fully present to *THIS*, without attachment, is a life fully lived. To love your enemies while recognizing that there are no enemies, to swim in the ocean as the Ocean—this is the mystery, wonder, and beauty of word made flesh. *THIS* is God.

When God is seen as *THIS*, the arguments between theism, atheism, nontheism, polytheism, or any other term with that root word get a little silly. Does God exist? Of course not, any God worth his salt could not possibly be

36. Matthew 25.

confined to a human idea like "existence"! But neither could one accurately say that God doesn't exist because "nonexistence" is also a concept of its own, far too limited to apply to an infinite and ineffable *THIS*. [37]

When I speak of God, I'm not speaking of being or nonbeing or both or neither. Borrowing the apophatic (or negative) language style of the Eastern Orthodox, who recognize that anything spoken of God is inherently incorrect, I might say something like, "God is All." God is not All. God is not not All. Hindus and Vedantists say *neti, neti* (not this, not that). Taoism states that the Tao that can be told is not the eternal, true Tao. Judaism understands that God's name, YHWH, is ineffable and therefore is not spoken. The mystics from every major tradition know of this unspeakable, unquantifiable, unabstractable nature of truth in their marrow.

THIS is God. Allah. Elohim. Huwa. Ishwar. Bhagavan. Brahman. Ram. Shangdi. Cheon-ju. Deus. Dios. Bahá. Abba. I Am. Call him what you want. Different names are used in different ways with different people. Just look at me! My audience calls me Gungor. My dad calls me Gil. My mom calls me Mick. My childhood friends call me Mike. Their parents call me Mikey. Most of my friends from my twenties call me Michael. Ram Dass called me Vishnu Dass (more about that in the next chapter). Most of my friends in Los Angeles call me Vish. My wife calls me Monk. Amelie calls me Dad. Lucie calls me Dadda. I should be so lucky to have so many names. Each represents stories, memories, and love formed of different shapes and stripes. Why should God have fewer names than I do?

Of course, many of us are not okay with that level of cosmopolitan universalism. When my daughter Amelie was five, I told her some of these other names for God that other people use. She wasn't thrilled about that. When I

---

37. Though some might find this open relationship with theological language frustrating or confusing, it excites me. For me, it's sort of the theological equivalent of Oprah's, "You get a car! And *you* get a car!" If the lack of precision bothers you, please feel free to dismiss it or just focus on your own car.

asked her why, she responded, "How would you like it if I called you 'Hideous'?" I had a good laugh at that, but the truth is that many of us hear the language and metaphors of other cultures and feel the same way as my kindergartner did. To many Christians, the multiarmed, colorful, or animalistic gods of Hinduism look scary and demonic. To many Buddhists, the eating of the body of Christ and drinking of his blood in Christianity seems barbaric. To many Protestants, Catholics are guilty of blasphemous idolatry by praying to Mary. I think much of this aversion to the religious expressions of others occurs for the same reason that a lot of Mexican people tend to like their food served a bit spicier than your average British person might—we tend to like what we are used to.

At this point of my life, I enjoy a wide variety of words, names, and metaphors for the Divine, like I enjoy a good fusion cuisine. As such, my use of the word *God* no longer comes with a bunch of necessary mythic attachments—it does not necessarily exclude or include an omnipotent, supernatural being, but I would assume that any being that exists would still exist within the ultimate and infinite context that is *THIS*. My view does not presume "we" are "real" or "simulated" or whether there is an infinite multiverse or a single, finite universe, but it does assume that there is no fundamental divide between the creator and the work of the creator. It does not exclude or include any view of an afterlife, but it does not place the imaginary construct of a human "I" on the great white throne of Heaven, so any sort of afterlife would still be seen as a temporary story and a condition and continuation of illusion, within the fundamentally storyless and seamless All.

God, for me, is a name for the nonduality that is beyond such categories as existence or nonexistence, matter or nothingness, real or imagined. God is All in All, beginning and end as they are now. Ey[38] is immanence and transcendence; form and void. She is nothingness

---

38. Spivak gender-neutral pronoun.

and everythingness. He is movement and stillness; eternal present. The here and now. Ne[39] is Alpha and Omega. Like I've said, all language fails miserably when you start trying to talk about this infinite [ ] because the words themselves are coming out of It and will always fall short of encompassing even a fraction of hir,[40] because there can be no meaningful fraction of infinity—a word that is itself a tiny sizzle of sound, a moment of vapor.

Still, I love speaking of my Self.

Why use so many pronouns? If I'm not limiting God to a cartoonish being in the sky, why bother with religious language at all? Because, remember, calling the great Blank Space or Void, which is beyond thought or understanding, an "it" or "the universe" is every bit as mythic as calling "him" "Zeus." I enjoy using a broad tapestry of pronouns and metaphors in order for the language to remain fluid and unstuck in any sort of dead or boundary-creating fundamentalism. Even if these words do come with the risk of minimizing ultimate reality into something that can be thought of and spoken, this broad tapestry of myth and metaphor can be a wonderful canvas to paint on, a fantastic backyard within which to play hide and seek.

The nonduality at the heart of the metaphors of many of the great Eastern traditions (especially Hinduism) have given me a taste for the [   ]-personifying myths again. To me, the union that they offer between the ideas of me and the idea of the ultimate or divine not only eliminates the inherent egocentrism, along with all of the shame, fear, and suffering that it engenders, but they can turn *THIS* into *thou* or *I* or *we* or whatever happens to make all of this feel more alive, more personal, more beautiful.

To experience the sun as a "her" on my skin can feel richer and more intimate than considering the sunlight a lifeless "it." To experience the Ground of Being as a living and present *thou* rather than a mere *that* can help one feel the music of the All in what seems to be a truer way. Any

39. Another gender-neutral pronoun.
40. Gender-neutral pronoun.

noun or pronoun we try to assign to ultimate reality will be too small, so why not use language that sparks the heart and imagination and that is as personal as our experience of ultimate reality feels?

It seems to me that by holding our sacred language more loosely, we have more space within which to play. If we could, for instance, find a healthy balance between the ego worshipping so common in the Christendom of the West and the potential ego negation of the more destructive social structures like India's caste system or China's human rights–violating aspects of communism in the East, I think there could be some beautiful music to be made. In the tension between these ancient stories, I think there are some inspiring harmonies to be discovered. Here, at these intersections, we can tell stories that include the small sense of "I" with all of its memories, stories, and personality, and in telling these stories well, we can provide a more just and equitable reality for the infinite differences within nonduality in which to dance together.

But we don't have to cling to or become attached to these stories to the degree where we become trapped inside them—where the boundaries of our skin are felt to be the true end of any "I am-ness." To experience *THIS* as God is to experience the bliss of loving and serving God without the fear and suffering of feeling separate from God. To think of God as *THIS* allows us to transcend and include the sacred cows of theists, atheists, and nontheists alike, giving us common ground upon which to converse. To see that *THIS* is God is to realize that we are home. We don't have to go anywhere or do anything to be in the heart of God. You're already here. You're already it.

THIS Is Awareness
Maui (2017)

I am loving awareness.
I am loving awareness.
I am loving awareness.

I let the mantra wash over me as I walk down the country road near Ram Dass's house in Maui. I'm on a private retreat with him and am playing with the mantra that he has given to me. The cool January tropical air is enlivening after so much sitting in silence. I walk the lane as mindfully as I can, repeating the mantra with every breath.

I am loving awareness.
I am loving awareness.

I think of how lucky I am to be on a retreat at Ram Dass's house. It would be hard to overstate how important his life and work has been to me. After the shit show that had played out in 2013–14, I had become a bit numb to the world emotionally. Even though I was much more grounded internally than I had ever been before the spa, everything in my life had been falling apart, and I felt that I had wasted so much of my life and energy on a foolish and useless belief system. When I came across the teachings of Ram Dass, they were like water for my parched soul.

Ram Dass, formerly known as Richard Alpert, had been a professor at Harvard in the '60s. He and Timothy Leary became famous for getting fired for their controversial experimentation with LSD. After his ousting from academia, Richard went on a spiritual quest to India, met his guru, Neem Karoli Baba (known also as Maharaj-ji), and his life changed. He ended up becoming a prominent spiritual sage and teacher in the '70s, '80s, and '90s. Then in 1997, he experienced a nearly fatal stroke that changed his life yet again. Today, Ram Dass is in his eighties. He needs constant care for his health, and he can't speak nearly as quickly or clearly as he used to be able to, but you should see his eyes. There's so much love in those eyes.

I am loving awareness.
I am loving awareness.

I continue to walk, slowly and mindfully down the rural lane near his house that leads down to the ocean. It is quiet but for the occasional birdsong or chirping insect. I slow the mantra down even more, so that the "I am" stands on its own before the "loving awareness" completes the phrase. I am not used to mantra meditation. I've always been more of a sit down and focus on your breath kind of meditator, but Ram Dass recommended it, so I'm giving it a go. And enjoying it so far.

In my first meeting with Ram Dass after arriving in Maui, he told me about how hard it was for his ego after his stroke, particularly when he was on stage. He used to be able to use his verbal acuity to take a room wherever he wanted to go. I've heard a good amount of those old recordings, so I knew how masterfully he could own a room with his wit and charm. He told me that he lost all of that with the stroke. He told me that now the best he can do if they wheel him out onto a stage is just love everyone. That's all he's got left. And he's so grateful for that. He thinks of the stroke as a great grace given to him by Maharaj-ji, who Ram Dass sees as his doorway to God, manifesting as everything and everyone.

Ram Dass entered my life at the perfect time. I had been meditating a lot more, and his teachings gave me language to things that I had experienced that I had never heard articulated so beautifully and heartfully. At the time, some of it was pretty out there and woo-woo for me, but I enjoyed how it stretched me. My reductionistic lens of viewing the world had become smaller than my experience of the world, and I was tired of reducing reality to the provable, testable, or perceivable. The more I listened to Ram Dass, the more I felt my heart opening up to the mystery within it all.

I am loving awareness.
I am loving awareness.

The country lane bends and a beautiful farmhouse appears. There are sprawling fields of long green and yellow grasses, the wind gently granting them movement. I feel the words coming straight from my heart to my lips.

I am loving awareness.
I am loving awareness.

I experience each step, each breath as a manifestation of love. I recall the new name that Ram Dass had just given me while we sat together in his study. He had been telling me how different his life was today than when he was called Richard Alpert. He said that name almost felt like a different incarnation to him at this point. I had told him some of my story already and I agreed that I too felt like an entirely different person than I used to. The name *Michael Gungor* sometimes felt like some other person. It was a brand, a Google search query that yielded bizarre and inaccurate results of my life. He asked me what kind of name I would like to have. I laughed and said I didn't know.

He had leaned back and closed his eyes.

I waited with bated breath. Was this really happening? I saw that I had constricted a bit and let it go, finding my breath. Becoming more present in my body.

Vishnu. He said in a whisper. He opened his eyes. They were beaming with joy.

Vishnu Dass.

Whoa. What would my Christian music fans on Facebook think of that one?

Still, something about the name resonated in my body. Vishnu Dass. He told me it meant servant of God.

God. I just couldn't get away from that word could I? Growing up, God was everything. In 2012, I had let God go. But apparently, He/She/It/They/I stayed around anyway.

Ram Dass smiled with the joy of a little boy. I couldn't help but smile back. We just sat there together for a while. I got lost in those wildly loving eyes of his that were somehow also mine, and we just shared each other's presence. Eventually, he began to talk about the moment. He slowly called out various happenings in our environment. The breeze coming in the window. The warmth of the sun. The airplane overhead. The flowers. The ocean. His slow pace brought a peace and depth to that moment that is hard to describe. Then he looked at me and said, "When you burrow deep enough into a moment, that's Vishnu."

Ah. I loved that.

He went on to tell me that he saw in me a man who had spent a lot of time living in my mind, but that he also saw me making an effort to live more in my heart. He told me about how when I can live in both, that's the essence of Vishnu—the creative dreamer of the world.

As I continue to get closer to the farmhouse, I wonder what I will do with that name. No way in hell my mom would call me that. But something about it feels so right. It feels like a new start. Vishnu Dass doesn't bring up any of the theological or identity baggage that my Christian name, Michael Gungor, does in my mind. But I also would never want to make Vishnu Dass its own ego game by thinking that it's important or necessary. Nor would I want to hurt my family or be guilty of some sort of cultural appropriation with a name like that. I don't know, I'll figure it out later.

I am loving awareness.
I am loving awareness.

Suddenly, a pit bull dashes towards me from the farmhouse, barking, mad and sounding thirsty for blood. Adrenaline shoots through my body as my heart begins to race. There's a fence between us, but it's not tall. This beast looks like it could easily jump over that thing and tear my throat out. It runs along the fence, snarling and barking. Frightened, I look around for a defensive weapon of some kind. I find a large rock. I look at the bloodthirsty, snarling dog with the rock tightly in my hand.

Don't you dare, or I will crush your skull, you fucking dog.
I take a breath.

"I am loving awareness," I whisper again. And then I laugh, the stone dropping back to the pavement.

· · · · ·

"When I consider your heavens, the work of your fingers, the moon and the stars, which you have set in place, what is mankind that you are mindful of them, human beings that you care for them?"
(PSALM 8:3–4)

I always have liked that passage in the Psalms. Ever since I was a kid, I always loved looking into the sky and feeling tiny. But one thing I failed to notice for a long time was the whole "fingers" thing. Throughout the Bible, people talk about the face, hands, and feet of God. God sits on a throne (with his butt?). He dances (with his legs?). He wears a robe and has hair like "wool." I suppose it's not that surprising that the human ego would imagine the infinite creative energy of the entire universe as a big human in the sky, fingers and all; still, it's pretty funny when you think about it. It's only slightly less on the nose than if a guy named Brian with red, curly hair who always wore Led Zeppelin T-shirts started a religion with a deity named Brian who happens to have red, curly hair and always wears Led Zeppelin T-shirts. (I wonder if there are any alien civilizations out there who have sacred texts about how the whole world is held in God's Zorgoplasm. Or how his giant, third antenna undulates on its hyperpod like the great Flergies of the Mt. Binglehorn. *The Word of our Lord. Thanks be to God!*)

Why is it that we so quickly personify and anthropomorphize God? I think it might have something to do with the reason that my dog, Willa B. Huckleberry Jones Gungor, launches into a frenzy of tail-wagging euphoria every time I greet her enthusiastically, regardless of whether I've been gone for ten minutes or a month—these mammal brains of ours were made to need each other. Experiments have shown that we literally depend on physical touch to survive. The need for attention and affection is wired deep into our brains because our survival and reproductive success is largely dependent on a good enough place in our social group. With that in mind, it makes sense why so many people would find comfort in the idea of a humanish ruler of the universe, the King of Kings, who not only is aware of me but who loves me. The leader of the pack is on my team. That's a powerful idea for us evolved, social apes.

One of the most-often sung church songs in the world is about how "our God" is "greater" and "stronger" than any others. I always found this to be odd, as typical Christian orthodoxy is not polytheistic. Who were these other gods we were comparing God to? Admittedly imaginary beings? Was "God, you're better than the tooth fairy!" really saying much? It made me wonder if perhaps the song (and the entire worship service) wasn't so much about God as it was about affirming to ourselves that our tribe was better than their tribe. Maybe "my dad can beat up your dad" wasn't ever really about either dad.

In the same way, maybe most (or all) of our religious beliefs, images, and practices are really more about us than God. This is just one of the problems in saying something like "*THIS* is awareness"—we are still projecting a conceptual model of a human experience (awareness) onto the rest of reality as a whole. So, of course, saying "*THIS* is awareness" is not quite true. But it's also not quite false. To explain what I mean, I'd like to ask you a question that is not usually asked in polite society:

Are your fingernails conscious?

If you are steeped in the mainstream, secular, mythic worldview of what Alan Watts called the "Fully Automatic Universe,"[41] you may answer no. At least, not by themselves. There are no neurons in fingernails. Fingernails, as far as we can tell, do not think or dream or have any separate sense of self from the rest of the body. But fingernails are part of the body, are they not? And if it is not the entire body that is conscious, what exactly in the body is conscious? The brain?

From what we can tell, human brains are what give rise to thoughts, and thoughts are the basis of what we consider to be "consciousness," so most of us would probably answer

---

41. According to Watts, the Fully Automatic Universe is modernity's updated version of the Genesis-based, Judeo-Christian creation myth. In the new, post-Christian secularism, natural laws replace divine fiats and physics and formulas replace the sovereign, powerful Word of God, but in both versions of this Genesis-based myth, the divide remains between humans and their source, between laws of nature and nature itself, between us and the universe that we study.

"yes, human brains are conscious." This would, of course, presume that the brain has not been puréed in a blender. One would presume that the brain in question is living and properly attached to a functional body. Even though the consciousness that occurs within the brain depends on the physical structures of the brain, those physical structures of the brain and the nervous system in which it is a part also depend on the skeletal, muscular, circulatory, pulmonary, and digestive systems of a living human body—including fingernails. All of these systems depend on and operate along with all sorts of other things—sunlight and vitamins and minerals and gravity and whatever the hell "dark energy" is—not to mention the social or collective consciousness in which any individual consciousness is rooted. In other words, it is impossible to draw a line around anything, whether it be a brain, body, species, or planet and say "this is all that is needed for conscious awareness to exist." Your thoughts and feelings are not just a product of gray matter, they are the stuff of family dynamics and cultural norms and supernovas and giant asteroids and possible alien civilizations. All of that has to be for all of this to be. You can't separate a rock in your driveway from everything that makes up your own consciousness any more than you can your own brain. It all goes together. The universe is, at least, conscious if you are conscious because you are the universe. If any of it is conscious, All of it is the very body of consciousness.

This doesn't mean that rocks think about things on their own. They don't, and neither do you. What you think of as your thoughts is simply all of *THIS* being what it is—the sun, the moon, the stars, your mind, and yes, your fingernails.

This removal of boundary lines between things and events does not feel natural to someone whose world is painted with the colors of assumed separateness. This sort of talk can sound like new-age drivel or sloppy, wishful thinking.[42] But if you dare to seriously question the

42. In modernity, the truth is often thought of as being undesirable—"the cold facts," "the hard truth," etc. But why are we so sure that this should be the case? How masochistic are we as a species that we so commonly assume that the truest things will be the worst possible things?

orthodoxy of separateness with any degree of diligence, it becomes quite clear that our culture's "common-sense" view of a fragmented reality is a construct and nothing more. And while useful to a degree, it is a construct that can only "explain" reality to a certain depth.

Think of a theist who can answer *almost* every question. Why does the earth spin? Gravity. And why does gravity exist? Well, God wills it so. If you then ask why God exists or who wills for Him to be so, you have found the end of the chain, that loop at the bottom of every story that comes back to itself as its own source of authority—God wills God to be so. In the same way, the atheists and other believers of the Fully Automatic Universe myth may reason with you that an infinite number of monkeys typing on an infinite number of typewriters for an infinite amount of time would eventually type every book humankind has ever written, so no there is no great mystery to existence—no God needed. But if you ask them where all the typewriting monkeys (physical laws, chaos, or potential) came from, they must face the self-reinforcing loop at the end of their own story—the typewriters, monkeys, and anything else needed for the process of apparent order emerging from chaos simply exist without explanation.

Those bewitched by their myths to the point of believing them to be unquestionably true from every angle are unable to see to the limited borders and usefulness of their own stories. For the theist, there is no need to consider any underlying meta-reality that allows God to exist and intervene in the universe without actually being the universe. For the believer in the Fully Automatic Universe myth, there is no need to see how randomness is a concept useful for insurance companies, lottery tickets, scientists, and casinos, but ought not be thought of as the true Nature of *THIS*.[43]

To think of any of *THIS* as ultimately being limited to any human word—random, sacred, meaningless, created,

---

43. Calling the ultimate nature of *THIS* random isn't exactly right—any more than saying a beehive is in the key of C minor. C minor is a greater abstraction than the concrete reality of a beehive, and the idea of randomness or meaninglessness is a greater abstraction than the concrete reality of isness.

conscious, chosen, etc.—will always be a reduction of
reality into a mere conceptual and anthropomorphic model
of that reality. These words are all constructs of the human
mind swimming in myth. Dirt, as far as we know, doesn't
find its own existence meaningless. The moon wouldn't
self-identify as an atheist or secularist. The concept of *matter*
is as mythic as the concept of *spirit*. The concept of *acciden-
tal* is as based in human story as the concept of *created*. To
think of the universe as a lifeless *it* is every bit as mythical
as calling it a living She, a personal I Am, or an infinite
stack of tortoises.

Of course, that doesn't mean that all myths are equal
in their outcome or fidelity to any possible objective reality.
The theory of relativity is most likely going to be far better
for plotting the launch of a satellite into space than the
fundamentalist Christian Gap Theory of creationism,
but whether we are journaling about lordship or writing
dissertations on quantum gravity, all of us are still just
telling stories. And for me, when I look at the consequences
of a civilization that sees and understands nature as a lifeless
it—a dumb, unconscious, random collection of *things* to be
consumed, plundered, and dominated at our pleasure—I
think we might do well as a species to allow ourselves to
learn some lessons from some of the more ancient stories
that treat nature with more reverence, even if that comes at
the cost of needing to apply a little anthropomorphism into
the mix here or there.

People who live in the world of concrete and
smartphones do not often have the same sort of connection,
sensitivity, and awareness of the environment that sustains
them as people who live among the trees and the mountains
and the deserts do. We think and speak of nature very
differently than many indigenous peoples and other
nonindustrialized populations have, and in many ways, both
we and our environment suffer for it. We feel like visitors
in our own home—alienated, isolated, and afraid. Rather

than flowing with the rest of Earth, we fight it, subdue it, conquer it. In relation to the planet, we, as a species, end up acting more like a cancer than a caretaker.

Every parent knows that feeling when you find out that the "it" of sperm and an egg becomes a "she" or a "he." How we think about Mother Earth determines how we treat her. Thinking of the universe as unconscious or unaware feels a bit degrading to me at this point—sort of like calling a baby an "it." Saying "*THIS* is awareness" or "*THIS* is fundamental consciousness" may be too small and limited for the ultimately ineffable *THIS*, but it certainly is not too grand, idealistic, or beautiful.

I've found that when I let go of the old ego guards afraid of being too superstitious or foolish according to the rules of the dominant culture around me, and I simply witness reality in loving awareness—I can feel how reality includes the seeing.

If we are conscious, the universe is at least as conscious as we are because we *are* the universe. If I can inhabit a space where I am loving awareness, the universe is at least loving awareness.

But is this just wordplay? Maybe. Still, why does gravity keep doing what gravity does? Why do cells keep dividing? Why does everything keep *being*? Does this not imply some sort of fundamental awareness or perception? How could one magnet pull on another if those pulls weren't somehow "aware" of each other? I realize that saying this is anthropomorphizing nonhuman objects, but what's the alternative? Imbuing the living Earth with the characteristics of a dead machine? Is that really better or more accurate? Also, are we so sure that when we talk about human "awareness" that we aren't doing the exact same thing of assigning more "personifying" story there than what is actually happening? Are we so sure that what we think of as "consciousness" or "awareness" isn't simply neurons being neurons, gravity being gravity, poles attracting or repelling poles?

Within the story of "*THIS* is awareness," spiritual practice becomes about not constricting awareness so fiercely into a fragmented ego story. Whether it is a breath, candle, note of music, or a mantra like *I am loving awareness*, focusing on a point of concentration can help quiet the thoughts and the myths that they are based in. This sort of practice can eventually silence the ego and melt one's experience into the presence of the source of that loving awareness. In this awareness, everything *is* awareness. Everything is fundamental consciousness. The table is being a table. The candle is being a candle. My mind is being a mind. Each and all occupying their place on the dance floor, following the steps perfectly.

Sight becomes God seeing Godself. Hearing becomes the music hearing itself. When we stare up at the stars, we are peering down into the depths of our own being. When our awareness is not turned against itself in the futility of its aversion to *THIS*, it becomes clear and open, like an endless blue sky. Thoughts and feelings come and go, but we do not feel imprisoned by them. We do not get caught in the loops of self-doubt, the fear of death, or the futility of striving, but simply rest in our most fundamental essence that is pure awareness. In the deepest place of this pure and loving awareness, there is no separation between subject and object. There is nobody watching and nothing being watched. It's just all being *THIS*.

The effect that this realization can have on the body/ mind of a human being is nothing short of life changing. There was a famous and relatively cruel set of experiments conducted by a man named Harry Harlow in the '50s and '60s, where baby monkeys were taken from their mothers and offered false "surrogate mothers" made of either cloth or wire. The monkeys who were given cloth mothers to cuddle with did far better emotionally and socially than those given wire mothers. In fact, given a choice between a wire mother who offered milk, and a cloth mother who did not, baby monkeys overwhelmingly still preferred the cloth mothers. I wonder what happens to a mammal who believes that she lives in a universe that, at its heart, does not see or love her. Would she not feel some sort of fundamental dread or fear about her existence? Wouldn't she be willing to do almost anything to fix that fundamental disconnect between her and her source? How much happier and content could she be if she could come to feel that the whole of things is not simply a cold, loveless math equation, but her very aware and loving mother?

So many of us are always stressed out, always calculating our place in the social order, always wondering if we are going to be okay.

If you are wondering if you are seen—you are. If you are wondering if you are loved—you are. Your existence is the All loving and dreaming you up from dust to the nanosecond. If you are afraid that this universe is a cold, loveless place, don't be. Those are just scary stories people told you. You are perfectly safe. The universe is, at least, aware because your loving awareness is the universe itself.

When my perspective shifts from wanting to be seen and loved to realizing that I am all of the loving awareness in the cosmos, those voices in my head that tell me that I need to find a way to climb the ranks in the tribe suddenly become quiet. That artist whom I used to be jealous of . . . that's *my* genius too. That guy who got the promotion instead of me . . . that's *our* promotion. I have nothing to be afraid of because what is there to be afraid of that I am not?

> *I am loving awareness.*
> *I am loving awareness.*
> *I am loving awareness.*

THIS Is Love

"He is a [sane] man who can have tragedy
in his heart and comedy in his head."
—G. K. CHESTERTON

I met her near the pier in Santa Monica. It was late, and she was crying hysterically. Sometimes, parts of my body still instinctually react to strangers' bodies as though they were separate somethings to be feared, pitied, or avoided. But not this time. This time, this stranger felt like she was my mother, my very own heart. My friend, Mike (Science Mike), and I approached her, asking if she was okay. She was beside herself. Her breath smelled of alcohol; her dress was tattered and torn. She told me that she had just hit someone.

That familiar sense of separateness peeked its head out. Did I need to be worried here? This woman was obviously not well and not sober. Was she dangerous? She asked me what was wrong with kids these days. She had promised herself she would never hit a child again. But only moments ago, she had. All she had wanted, she said, was a little help getting down the stairs in the park. I told her I was so sorry for what she was going through and encouraged her to take a few deep breaths to help her calm down a bit.

As she breathed, I noticed her hands. One hand was trying to hold her torn dress in place over her body. On the other, she wore a black wrist brace. On the weathered fingers that extended from the brace, she wore several jeweled rings. Standing there wailing next to the pier, filthy, drunk, and homeless, late on a Monday night, our Mother still longed for dignity. She still wanted to be seen as beautiful. Looking at her, I could see that she was, but I didn't know how to tell her that without coming across as weird or creepy. Her sobs gradually began to slow as her breath deepened. She told us she was thirsty. Could we please get her some water? Yes, we could do that. Could we please help her sit down somewhere while she waited? Her health wasn't good, and she had a hard time getting around by herself. Yes, we could do that, too. We led her to the bus stop. She thanked us and begged us to please come back with the water. She really was so thirsty. We promised we would be back shortly.

We found a McDonald's that was open late and full of the sorts of interesting characters that hang around the Santa Monica pier in the middle of the night. I thought about my life. My clean and comfortable house. My family and friends. I live within a bubble of privilege that such a small percentage of human beings have ever experienced. I ordered a bottle of water and some french fries.

We walked back with the goods and found her seated in the same place we had left her. She had calmed down a lot since we left. She thanked us for coming back and asked if we could help her with one other thing—could we just help her find a spot to lay down so she could go to sleep?

I felt a pang of sadness through my chest. It was rough out here for a sick, elderly woman with nothing but a torn dress and some jewelry on her fingers. There were drunk, stoned, and shady-looking characters everywhere. I had seen a couple rats dart across the grass just a few minutes before. I couldn't let her sleep here. What could I do? Could I get her a hotel room or something? Money was a bit tight for us as a family, but if we had to, we could afford it. But, no, I had heard what can happen if you try to provide hotel rooms for homeless people. Mike knew firsthand. He had once tried to get a few rooms for some people he met on the street who had nowhere to stay. The hotel had not only refused but had called security and had the rejected guests escorted off of the premises. The manager warned Mike that if he ever tried something like that again, he would be permanently banned from the hotel as well.

That may sound cruel at first glance, and maybe it was. But when you try to imagine the scenario from a hotel manager's perspective, it's complicated. After all, hotels operate their businesses on the necessary assumption that the guests will not destroy the rooms or steal things from them, and how could they ensure such a thing from someone who could not take enough care of themselves to maintain consistent shelter? What if the person was mentally ill or addicted to something and ended up stealing from the hotel, wrecking the room, or scaring other guests? How could the hotel ensure a nondisastrous stay from people with no credit cards or other assets to guarantee that they will behave responsibly?

The woman with the torn dress pointed to a spot on the ground near a bush and asked if it was too wet there. I reached down and touched the grass. It was a little damp. She asked if the sprinklers would come on there in the middle of the night. We didn't know. Out of the corner of my eye, another rat darted from one bush to another, probably hunting for more food scraps from the beach visitors. I looked at the woman's face, my eyes burning with tears. It wasn't that I simply felt sorry for her. In that moment, I could feel that her heart was my heart. I saw her. I loved her. I felt no distance or separation from her. She was my mother. My sister. Myself. My God. And, my God, it hurt.

Could I get her to a shelter? It was already so late; the shelters were probably all full or closed now, and I didn't know of any shelters around there to check anyway. There were so many homeless people around, I couldn't imagine that there was an easy fix to be found. Still, my mind continued to spin, trying to imagine a possible solution to this woman's predicament. I wanted to take away her suffering. I wanted her to be back with her family. I wanted her to not have hit those children. But deep down, I knew that I couldn't fix this. This was not a simple problem that ended with one woman not having anywhere to sleep that night. I was walking into a vast matrix of problems that involved an entire lifetime of patterns and stories, of systems and generations and layers of complexity that I simply had no way of getting to the bottom of on a Monday night while holding a bag of french fries in my hands. As much as I wanted to, I couldn't fix this. But was that just a cop out? A justification of my own privilege?

She reached out her braced hand to me and asked me to help her lie down.

But how could I do that? If my actual mother visited my house, would I allow her to sleep on the damp ground with the rats while I slept inside in my warm king bed? Of course not! I'd rather sleep in the grass myself. But what could I do? Drive her back to my house and ask my wife to let her sleep in our bed with us? Have her sleep with our little girls downstairs? That didn't feel wise. I felt so powerless.

I took her hand and lowered her frail body onto the cold, damp earth. I couldn't keep the tears contained in my eyes anymore. I quickly wiped my face so she wouldn't see and feel ashamed. She asked if I could open the bottle of water for her. I opened it and handed it back. Still holding the brown paper McDonald's bag, I awkwardly asked her if she wanted any french fries. She politely declined as another couple of rats scampered a few feet away.

. . . . .

To allow the prickly edges of the human ego to melt into the infinite ocean of loving awareness in this world is often an exceedingly painful endeavor. It is much easier to keep one's rib cage closed, one's heart small and manageable. True union with *THIS*, after all, isn't only to be one with the stars, flowers, saints, and sages, but also with the criminals, bigots, diseased, and despised. How can a judge or juror send a man to death row when he knows the convicted is his brother? How can a soldier fight in a war when she knows that national identities are nothing but stories? How can an activist who understands the severity of human-induced climate change continue to travel, work, eat, and live when he knows how all of it only worsens the problem? How can a loving and awake parent take her children to Disneyland knowing the pitfalls of capitalism, the rampant patriarchy of so many Disney stories, and that the money could easily be spent instead on giving other children access to clean water? And how, in God's name, can I lay our Mother down in the grass to sleep with the rats? In other words, trying to love in a world like this is a mess.

I drove by my daughter's school today and noticed a mural on one of the exterior walls. It was a series of ocean waves, and it said, "You, I, we . . . are love!" I thought it was lovely and it made me wonder for a moment why I am spending so much time writing this book when that's a pretty good summation of all I have to say. But it also made me think how easily and casually love is usually thought of in our culture—perhaps especially in LA! It sounds so nice and romantic to say that we are all love. All we need is love! Love is the answer! This sort of thing is everywhere in progressive culture.

Every creed, race, gender, and orientation is welcome at this taco truck!

In my neighborhood, the messages of love and inclusion are literally stenciled on the sidewalks. The concept of love is cool. It's also a potent concept to unite a group and enable them to feel superior to others.

We are so much more loving than those assholes!

But the reality of love isn't always so convenient. Extending love to everything and everyone at the end of a yoga session may be a wonderful thing to say, but to actually put that into practice is often a bloody, painful shit show because it involves knowingly accepting and even causing potential suffering for those you love. To buy a dog for your kid is to ensure their heart will be broken sometime in the next decade or two when their beloved dog dies. To sell all that you have and give it to the poor is to create the need for someone else to have to take care of your broke ass. Love is rarely as clean or simple as our greeting cards, love

songs, or rom-coms present it. To love one person is sometimes to break the heart of another. Love isn't all chocolate
and roses and strummed ukuleles. Love also sometimes
involves conflict, embarrassment, and bloody crosses.

And it is because of this complexity, I think, that
of these three stories I'm telling about the nature of
THIS, *THIS is love* presents perhaps the most poignant
opportunity to harmonize some of the thoughts from both
the ancient trees (Christianity, Hinduism, Buddhism, etc.)
and some of the newer sprouts (physics, integral theory,
post-structuralism, etc.) Thoughts that may, on the surface,
appear to be contradictory can find a harmony and synergy
within a topic like love, that has so much room for depth,
nuance, and even conflict. In this balance, perhaps we can
find ourselves loving *THIS* without being overwhelmed or
lost to feelings of hopelessness or futility.

Perhaps we could begin the fusing of some of these
meta-stories about love with the Christian notion of
love. "God is love" was and is, for me, the most powerful
declaration of the Christian tradition. That idea is at the
heart of the best expressions of Christianity throughout
history, and it is the reason that I never became anti-
religious, even as an atheist. For all that the biblical authors
got wrong about issues like gender, sexuality, or cosmology,
they got a lot right about love. There are few pieces of
writing that have been as important or impactful in my
own life as Jesus's Sermon on the Mount, St. Paul's famous
exposition about love in 1 Corinthians 13, or even some
of the verses in 1 John that equate loving God with loving
one's neighbor.

The Christian idea of incarnation and its relationship
to love is one of my favorite aspects of the faith. For God
so loved the world that he gave: himself. We humans are
always telling stories about the hero who kills all of his
enemies or the great ruler who brings glory to his people
through might, riches, and power, but in the Christian story,

the great omnipotent King of the Universe empties himself of his glory, splendor, and power and takes up residence in the screaming, vulnerable, body of a human baby being pushed through a stretched and bloody vulva. In this story, the King of Kings is not born in a palace to a Caesar, but in a manger to a teenaged refugee. In this story, Jesus claims identity not with the rich and powerful oppressors of his day, but with those who are on the underside of power. Children loved him. Prostitutes revered him. Religious leaders hated him. He taught people about loving one's enemies and taught that his true disciples would be known by their love. His radical life and message of love led to his brutal, state-sanctioned murder, even as he prayed with some of his final breaths, "Father, forgive them, for they do not know what they do." Then, in the story of his resurrection, love is shown to be the ultimate reality in the universe—more powerful even than death.

Here's a quote from Science Mike's (Mike McHargue is his real name) book, *Finding God in the Waves*,[44] about how meaningful the story of Christ's resurrection is for him in his experience of reality:

> One day, I will die, and in time my atoms will go back to being alive in something else. Much farther along the arrow of time, our own sun will explode and spread its essence across the sky. Our sun's dust will meet with other stars' remains and form new stars and planets of their own. The Universe itself exists in an eternal pattern of life, death, burial, and resurrection. It seems poetically appropriate that the Source of All would've left this divine signature on the fabric of reality.

When it is held with open hands rather than constricted into literalism and fundamentalism, I think the Christian story has the ability to inspire a tremendous amount of faith, hope, and love in the world today, as it has for nearly

44. Mike McHargue, *Finding God in the Waves: How I Lost My Faith and Found It Again through Science* (New York: Convergent Books, 2016).

two thousand years. Christian love has given us people like St. Francis, Dr. Martin Luther King Jr., Nelson Mandela, Rosa Parks, Dietrich Bonhoeffer, Corrie ten Boom, Henri Nouwen, and countless other inspiring, world-changing figures. Christian love has given us children's hospitals, needle exchange programs, and clean water for people without access to it. Christian love has clothed the naked, fed the hungry, and cared for countless widows and orphans throughout twenty centuries of history. The love that I have personally witnessed and experienced within the Christian community throughout my life made it impossible for me to not maintain some level of affection and gratitude for the Church, even when I let go of the Church's God.

Still, with all of the good that Christianity's notion of love has brought to the world, it seems to me that there is a fly in the ointment—a disjointedness at the heart of Christian theology that can sometimes limit the efficacy of its gospel. This disjointedness is, as we've seen, the egocentrism and assumption of separateness between God and his creation at the core of the Christian imagination.

To begin to understand why this is a problem when it comes to love, consider this scenario:

You fall head over heels in love with someone. You decide to take them on a nice date and tell them how you feel. One night, after eating together at an upscale restaurant, the two of you go on a romantic walk in the soft glow of the moonlight. When the mood feels just right, you stop walking, and turn to face your beloved. "I love you," you whisper for the very first time. Your darling smiles and then responds, "Thank you for telling me that. Honestly, I have no desire for you. I don't really feel like loving you, as you do nothing for me emotionally. But I am a Christian and believe strongly that it is my duty to love in a way that is ultimately selfless. Because of this, I think this may be a great opportunity to serve God and fulfill my Christian duties to live for the happiness of others and not myself. So, in selfless service and humble obedience to God, I say to you, my dear, I love you too!"

That's not really the stuff of romance novels. My guess is that you wouldn't be thrilled with that response. But why is that? Don't you want somebody to love you selflessly? To serve you and do what they think is right?

Now, let's go back to the "I love you" on the moonlight walk one more time, only this time, imagine they respond like this instead: "To be honest with you, there are a million reasons in my head why I shouldn't fall in love right now. But, with you, I can't help myself. I'm hooked. I need you. I desire you. I love you with every fiber of my being."

Which of the two responses would you prefer? The selfless response about duty or the selfish response about addiction and desire? Or here's another question: While making love to someone, would you rather have a partner who is moaning and writhing with the pleasure they are feeling in their own bodies, or someone who felt nothing for themselves, but dutifully and obediently offered pleasure to you as an act of selfless humility and compassion? These are easy answers for most of us because the truth is that we want people to be selfish in their love for us. Not *entirely* selfish to the degree that they don't actually love us or consider our needs and feelings, but also not selfless to the degree that they are merely principled automatons.

Love is most powerful when loving you *is* loving myself.

Think of the language we use to describe how it feels when we love someone. We feel *close* to them. We feel *connected* to them. In matrimony, two hearts are said to be joined as *one*. Two become one flesh. The experience of love is the experience of a reduced sense of emotional distance. Love brings us *together*. Absolute love is an absolute closing of any perceived distance—where your heart becomes my heart, your pleasure becomes my pleasure, your desire becomes my desire.

How can we ever truly love God or our neighbor (the primary commandments for the Christian as laid out by Jesus himself) if we remain fundamentally separated from both God and our neighbor? How could you love someone if there wasn't anything *in you* that *desired* to love them? And what desire of the self is not "selfish"? When a hero jumps in a freezing river to save a stranger, and you ask them why, they usually respond with something seemingly self-effacing like "it was just the right thing to do." Or "I didn't even think about it. I just did it." And that may be true. But why did they follow their instincts?

Why does the bird work so hard in building that nest for her eggs? Why do bees risk their lives day in and day out leaving their hive to gather pollen? For some abstract, philosophical notion of "the greater good?" Of course not; it is because they are following their instincts—their built-in desires. Whether someone's desires are to get as many likes as possible on a selfie or to serve the sick and the poor in an AIDS clinic in Calcutta, that person always and only acts because of their *own* desires, even if those desires are to fulfill someone else's desires. The idea of "selflessness" or "sacrifice" as it is marketed by purveyors of religious goods and services, is often just selfishness with a mask on—another way of stroking our ego by misunderstanding or ignoring our deepest desires to be better than other people. *Look at how selfless I am!* This is not to say that the acts of love that we often think of as "selfless" are always really just masked, ego-driven selfishness. What I am saying is that those who truly love others are not doing it at the expense of themselves, but as a fulfillment of themselves, a melding into the flow and connectivity of love that brings lover and loved closer together.

The fundamental separation at the heart of Christian theology between God and creation dooms the ideals of Christian love to ultimately be an untenable futility in its fullest aims. If my ego remains fundamental, I can never truly love anything but my own ego.

If I give all I possess to the poor . . . but do not have love, I gain nothing.

On the other hand, without the illusion of separateness, the act of loving one's neighbor or oneself can be seen as one in the same as the act of loving God. As my sense of ego dissolves into the All, there are no transactions, no gift or giver, no one to be loved or to do the loving. There is only Love.

The Problem of Evil

O ne other problem that comes up with the myth of Christian separateness in relation to the idea that *THIS is love* is the "problem of evil," which haunted me for so many years. Occupying a myth where God remained separate from his world, the sort of love that my heart felt drawn to was often overrun by the thoughts and questions in my head. I was often paralyzed with a sense of meaninglessness and futility that accompanied the questions about why this world is like it is. Why so much suffering? Why the holocaust and rape and entropy and the fact that all life has to kill in order to live? How could a good, all-powerful, and sovereign God allow such unthinkable amounts of evil and suffering to exist? How could *he* let this happen to *us*?

And here, I think we need to hear from some of the other trees in the forest in order to tell the story of *THIS is love* in the fullest way possible. In other ancient stories, the assumed distance between God and his creation that makes the problem of evil feel so relevant in the Christian and post-Christian myths, is experienced as an ultimately meaningless illusion. From the perspective of ultimate unity, after all, separation is only a temporary story—part of the romance and adventure of it all and not the final word. From this higher vantage point of Oneness, the problem of evil can be seen for what it really is—a problem of language.

As we have seen, there is no story that is fundamental to *THIS*. Stories are the seams of illusion that we sew into reality. They're the imaginary grid we lay out across the movement of the All, in order to label this and that. Before these lines are drawn, there is no perspective or experience. There is just the ocean, only the dance and movement of God. This is backstage, if you will, where all the actors take off their masks.

Here, there is no good, no evil, just *THIS*. Good and evil, like everything else, are born from the stories we tell.

For instance, is a wave crashing onto a beach evil? I would imagine you would say no. But what if you found out the waves at that beach were self-aware? What if that majestic wave that crashed to its demise had seen its own end coming and had feared it? What if you found out the wave's loved ones were now in mourning after their beloved friend, husband, and father wave had been viciously torn apart by the sand? Perhaps you might wonder what kind of ocean would allow waves to crash so violently against the shore like that?

Why is it that we do not consider it tragic for our cells to commit suicide for the sake of our body's survival or for our immune system to fight off viruses or virulent bacteria that have made their way into our bloodstream? Why do we not wonder about the justness of a composer who scored so many F notes yet so few F-sharps in that sonata or wail in lament as the sun disappears from our sight at the end of every day? It is because what we consider to be good or evil is always and only a matter of story.

In most of our stories, crashing waves don't matter. We don't sweat killing billions of bacteria every time we wash our hands, and giving hungry humans food is considered good because human life is considered more important than other kinds of life. But these are not the same stories we would tell if we were aliens from some other galaxy, super-intelligent bacteria, or self-aware philosopher waves staring back out at the ocean and thinking about the meaninglessness of waving.

This is another one of those truths that is admittedly a precarious undertaking to try to constrict into words

177

because it is possible for people with power and privilege to abuse ideas like oneness and the relativity of evil by minimizing the suffering of the people whom they oppress. It is not enlightenment for a slave owner to say, "Well I am the slave owner, but I am also the slave!" It is not enlightenment to turn an idea of fundamental unity into a perverted, watered-down version that really is masked oppression, erasure, gaslighting, or violence. To only take the abstract truth from nondual unity and to ignore the practical implications of the importance of differences is to miss the beauty of nondual realization entirely. Still, as a person who wrestled for years with the problem of evil, the stories that present God not as a Big Other, but as the Oneness expressed as All, have allowed me to see that the problem of evil that I used to wrestle with was simply the result of my assumption that God was somehow "other" than all of *THIS*. When the separation between my sense of self and my sense of God was erased, the question "Why does God allow evil?" became nonsensical.

When the Divine is seen not as an agent that stands apart from the world but instead the mystery expressed by and as the world, there are no victors or victims but God. *"From him, through him, to him are all things."*

But if there is any sort of awareness or love that is a fundamental aspect of the nature or essence of *THIS*, as I'm suggesting, why would existence include so much suffering? And, this is where post-structuralism comes to the rescue! (Don't worry, I won't hang out here long.) But post-structuralism helped reveal how our binaries (good/ evil, for example) are never quite as simple as we like to think. Each of those terms came from somewhere in history and shouldn't be lazily lumped together as though there were an actual structure in reality where good and evil can be thought of as real and equal opposites. In other words, when we start talking about ideas like good and evil, let's not oversimplify or assume too much about how those two concepts relate without careful examination of what we're getting at and where all of that came from.

Of course, fully delving into the concepts of good and evil philosophically is far too extensive of an endeavor for a book like this, but for our purpose, suffice it to say that we shouldn't simplify ideas like love, suffering, good, or evil to the point where we get permanently stuck on questions like, "How could existence be thought of as 'loving awareness' and yet still include all of this suffering?" The truth is that the opposing energies of yin and yang create a lot of room for paradox and tension, and these tensions are the only way that this universe can be this universe.

In this universe, what we think of as opposites always go together, even if their relationship is not as simple as our normal binary thinking might make it. There is no such thing as up if there is not also down. You can't have the joy of union without separation. There is no order without chaos. There is no bliss without suffering. All of it goes hand-in-hand, though not always in equal measure. Our normal mythic perspectives often force us into small thinking about these perceived opposites. We think of this event as good and that one as bad. Life is good. Death is bad. Happiness is good. Pain is bad. But, as we have seen, all of these opposites fit together as a necessary balance of flow within the All. You could never have one of these "positives" without all of the interconnected "negatives." Nor would you want to.

You might disagree with that last sentence at first. You might say something like, "I'll take unending bliss with no suffering please!" Okay. Imagine you could will yourself to have one uninterrupted orgasm of bliss for as long as you'd like. How long do you think you would enjoy that? Ten minutes? Ten hours? Ten years? A hundred thousand years? Two hundred trillion years? I would imagine whatever the number would be that you may overestimate how long you would enjoy it. I saw a TV show once where they showed this guy who has a medical condition where he spontaneously has dozens of orgasms every day. He was miserable. He was having orgasms during his grandpa's funeral. This poor guy lives his life in nearly constant suffering from too much pleasure.

If you take a moment and really try to imagine an existence of only uninterrupted eternal bliss, it becomes clear that such an imagined existence is an absurdity. What good is a glass of cold water without the thirst for it? What is life without death, creativity without entropy?

Looking at things through the Hindu lens for a moment, ask yourself this question: If you were an infinite, playful, and creative love, what game wouldn't you play, at least for a little while? After all, maybe in some segment of a multiverse, you (God) are playing other sorts of games where you don't forget that you are God. Maybe you are playing an infinite number of games in an infinite number of universes, where you experience bliss a billion years at a time while fully remembering that you are the infinite Godhead. But would you stop there? Is that all you would ever do? Or would you consider trying another game at some point? Maybe one where you go on adventures that make you afraid? Maybe some where you even forget you are you for a bit? As the Infinite, would you ever consider taking up residence as an evolved ape on a tiny speck of a blue gem suspended in space with a penchant for Chinese takeout and a nose that is a tiny bit off-center of your divine face? Maybe you would enjoy a game with some apparent randomness in it? Why wouldn't you? What would you have to lose? It all comes back to you in the end. Why not infinitely love that character and every variation possible of that character? Infinity leaves room for a lot of patterns to paint, a lot of love to express, a lot of songs to sing, a lot of journeys to take, and a lot of games to play.

If you were an infinite ocean, you would ultimately become an infinite amount of all possible waves. And why not? And who is the clay to say to the potter, "Why have you made me like this?"

When you shift your perspective to stay aware of this higher vantage point while remaining engaged in the stories of your experiences, all of the drama of life becomes less weighty. It's sort of like the experience of watching a good film, where on one plane of awareness you are fully experiencing the drama, but on another, you know you're watching a movie. If it's a particularly good film, you may get so caught up in the story that you momentarily forget you are watching actors performing in front of cameras. But very few people would ever get PTSD from watching a war scene in a movie. Because even if we are emotionally involved, something deep within us knows that it's actually going to be okay. Even if the character on the movie gets killed, we know deep down that the actor is not in real danger. It's just a movie, after all.

In the same way that it is possible to hold that the murder and suicide in Romeo and Juliet is *bad* while simultaneously saying that the play itself is *good*, it is possible to be involved in the drama and emotion of human life in a way where we get caught up in the story of suffering and fighting and working for good, but have a stillness inside of it all that knows deep down that all of it is story and at the deepest level, it is all perfect just as it is. It's possible to push back against death and entropy while seeing that death and entropy are a necessary part of the whole. It is possible to work for the Kindom[45] of God to manifest on earth while knowing deep down that it's already here. In this multiplaned awareness, we can see that all of *THIS* is love without losing our passion to bring more love into the world.

But what does it mean for all of *THIS* to be love? Isn't that just more anthropomorphic, sentimental woo? To see why I think saying *THIS is love* is a reasonable thing to say, let's hear from some of the other younger stories as well.

45. A name used in certain streams of feminist or liberation theology in lieu of the more patriarchal "Kingdom."

· · · · ·

Physics has unveiled the workings of a universe that is weirder than any of us could have ever imagined. For instance, nobody has ever been able to find any real *thing* at the bottom of anything. When you look out into the night sky, there are stars, but there's a whole lot of space between those stars. That's how everything is when you look close enough. The whole universe consists of all these little interconnected, empty, vibrating, floaty, magic swirls, or *wiggles*. The physical sense with which you're feeling this book in your hand right now gives you a sensation of something solid touching something solid, but that's an illusion. No "thing" ever touches any other "thing." What you feel as solidity is just forces repelling one another, or in Watts-speak, it's just wiggles wiggling.

This "solid" book is a wiggle made up of other wiggles—ideas, polymers, atoms made of stardust that were once in the lungs of a blue whale or the arm hair of Julius Caesar, etc. It's also a small part of other larger wiggles— the room you are in, the planet Earth, the Milky Way, etc. Quantum mechanics reveals that these fundamental wiggles aren't *things* but, like music, are relationships of vibration.[46] What we think of as a *thing* is simply our recognition of a temporarily repeating melody or motif within the notes.

Music has layers. You can listen to the bassist, or the violin section, or the lyrics, but it all goes together, and in a good piece of music, it all belongs. The tension, the resolution, the rise and fall, the noise and the silence, it all works together to form a cohesive whole.

When you look out at the world, with all its complexity, you are literally seeing vibration—seeing music. The leaves blowing in the trees—music. The clicking of the commuter's shoes on the tile floor of the train station. The sound of children playing in the park, the sound of the helicopter flying overhead, the Instagram feed of that annoying girl at work who is always posting

---

46. To once again quote the theoretical physicist Carlo Rovelli, "It isn't *things* that enter into *relations*, but rather relations that ground to the notion of *thing*." See Carlo Rovelli, *The First Scientist: Anaximander and His Legacy* (Bucks County, PA: Westholme Publishing, 2011).

pictures of her food—it's all music. Some of the notes are pleasant to the ear; some of them are grating. But together, they make up a symphony that includes all of the sophistication, subtlety, and beauty that you have ever experienced or imagined.

The whole universe is built of these little musical motifs within motifs. Integral theorist and philosopher, Ken Wilber, coined the word *holon* to speak of this phenomenon. The whole fabric of the universe consists of these "whole" systems that are also always a "part" of other whole systems. For example, an atom can be seen as a whole that transcends but includes other smaller parts, which are wholes in themselves consisting of other parts . . . and on and on it goes. There is no end in sight to these stacks of holons, either up or down. An atom is part of a molecule; which is part of a cell; which is part of a nervous system; which is part of a body; which is part of a biosphere; which is part of a planet; which is part of a solar system; which is a part of a galaxy; which is a part of the observable universe; which, as far as we know, could be a part of a divine being or some random dream in the brain of an elven goddess who is part of a computer simulation; which itself is part of a computer simulation; and so on and so on to infinity that is all an unforeseen consequence of a science experiment for some intelligent community of super-bacteria on the buttocks of a bonobo that is roughly the size of the Virgo Supercluster. My point is that we don't have any idea how far up or down these holons go, but this whole/part pattern does seem to be the way that the void manifests as form.

So what does any of this have to do with love? As we discussed earlier, love is the connection, the relationship, the desire that brings separate *parts* together into a new *whole*. When we experience love, we are getting swept up into some greater reality that transcends and includes our individual sense of self. I love my wife and my daughters, and in that experience of loving them, I feel caught up in something greater than my own ego. In love, it's not just me. And it's not just them. An us is born. Love joins disparate parts into a single, transcendent whole.

In physics, we see that subatomic particles join together in a sort of "relationship" with one another, thereby creating a new "we," or atom. Atoms are "attracted" to other atoms just as planets are to suns and galaxies are to other galaxies. In other words, there seems to be something fundamental within reality about connection and relationship. There is something about a negative charge that "desires relationship" with a positive one. There is something about gravity that pulls matter towards itself. Couldn't one say that is a form of "longing"? In this loose way of talking about objects in very human terms, one could say that the universe is made of love.

In saying that, I'm not saying that the universe is literally made of the human emotion of love. Conversely, the human emotion of love may simply be a clear manifestation of how things operate at the core of reality—connection, desire, and relationship.

What is it that keeps trees growing toward the sky? What is it that keeps every cell in your body working to keep you alive, living and dying for the greater good that is you, even if they don't understand that greater good themselves? Why not call that creative, organizing, and sustaining unity underneath it all love?

THIS is love.

Allowing myself to mix myths now, I can feel that the only true *I* is the One Dance underneath it all, the play between heaven and earth; the love between Father, Spirit, Son; the unity of Brahma, Vishnu, and Shiva; the mysterious dance of protons, neutrons, and electrons within an atom.

What holds the cloud floating in the blue sky? All of it. How many small particles and patterns of energy have to connect and cooperate to make that cloud appear as it did in your brain? All of them. All the energy in the whole universe has to take its place on the orchestra stage just for that particular cloud to appear like it does. That period at the end of the sentence had to happen just as it did for that cloud to appear like that. Not necessarily because one thing causes the other, but because everything in this universe goes along with everything else, just as every hair on your head goes with your hairstyle. Every ripple in the ocean is a necessary part of the pattern of energy that needed to exist within this moment for the ocean to be just what it is.

THIS is love.

By incarnating, God gets to experience having and loving a baby. Billions of times over. He gets to experience being a newborn baby. Billions of times over. It gets to be a sunrise and a viewer of a sunrise. She gets to compose every symphony, and listen to every performance of it. We get to build and witness the end of every empire, feel every victory and defeat of every battle. *I Am-ness* feels the pain of every tragedy and the happiness of every triumph. Playfulness gets to play. Story gets to be told. The ocean gets to feel the dramatic movement of every individual wave. And as any individual crest finally breaks upon the shore and flows back to it source, the great sea has already churned up a thousand new stories from the depths of its belly with the adamant joy of a child who screams in delight after being tossed into the air by her father—"*again!*"

How else would you have it?

In the film *Arrival*, one of the characters sees into the future and learns that if she has a child, she will lose that child in the future. She knows she will have her heart broken, and that it will hurt beyond her ability to bear. But she chooses to have the child anyway. She chooses to experience love, even though she knows that love comes with unbearable torture, concurring with that famous Alfred, Lord Tennyson quote: "Tis better to have loved and lost than never to have loved at all."

What else would infinite love do, other than love everything and everyone? What else would infinite creativity and playfulness do, but see through every perspective and incarnate into every possible narrative? What stories would Fearless Becoming be afraid of telling? With an infinite play chest, what arrangement of matter and space would go unexperienced or unloved?

Human culture has tended to value uniformity—in our society, which has historically leaned toward the male, the white, the able, and the normally gendered. But this is the uniformity of death—as all the living systems and variety within the body stop their movement and devolve into a dead heap of decomposing cells. *THIS* is so much more alive than *that.*

In the human family alone, God puts on wildly different hues of eyes, hair, and skin. *THIS is love* shows us that God is most importantly found where we have forgotten to look for him. He walks proudly in the culturally shamed bodies of the queer and the transgender. She sits in a wheelchair and lies dying in hospital beds. It's easy enough for many people to find God in churches, picturesque nature, or success. But there is a reason Jesus identified with the most overlooked and forgotten corners of our society. If you want to find God, you can always find him in prison, in a mental institution, or sleeping under a bridge.

Some forms of spiritual practice focus on transcending suffering—not being affected or weighed down by the grit of life. Other practices focus on incarnation and imma-nence—sharing in the stories and suffering of others. *THIS is love* creates room for the practice of both transcendence and immanence by allowing for the drama of a perceived "other," without losing sight of the fundamental unity be-tween "thou" and "I." Here, we don't have to get lost in the weeds of egocentric separation, but we can play in them. We can feel the full brunt of life and death without being incapacitated. We can enjoy the play without forgetting that the villains are just actors on a stage. We can fight for the liberation of the world from within our own unfolding liberation rather than from the despair, fear, and illusion of trying to change the world as an ego. *THIS is love* means life can be lived in the full light of day—not avoiding the pain, adventure, and romance of incarnation, nor missing out on the peace and contentment that comes in nondual realization. *THIS is love* means life—and life lived to the fullest as we brave the journey of walking in, with, and as God.

In this balance between perspectives, we can love the homeless woman, doing our best to serve her while also being angry at the systems that make her problems so complicated, all while knowing underneath it all that it is all perfect just as it is in *THIS*. We can work for shalom to come into the earth while knowing that it was already here the whole time. I think this is what it means to, as G. K. Chesterton put it, "have tragedy in our hearts and comedy in our heads."[47]

47. G. K. Chesterton, *Tremendous Trifles* (New York: Dodd, Mead & Co, 1909).

Free to Suffer

*"There's blood in your heart,
and Jesus is in the blood."*
—AMELIE GUNGOR
(three years old)

A few days ago, Lisa told me that our daughter Amelie recently asked her, "Momma, am I pretty?"

Tears immediately spilled down my cheeks. My heart felt like a nerve suddenly exposed to the air. Amelie, you see, is a gorgeous human being. She has the soul of a sage, the warmest smile, and those brilliant blues from her mother. She has no rational reason to be insecure in who she is. She's pretty, smart, hilarious, and talented. But she also lives in this world. She sees what our culture values. She sees the kind of women cast as leading ladies. She sees what sorts of faces get printed on the covers of magazines, which girls get followed around at school by all of the others. As hard as Lisa and I have tried to instill in Amelie how neither her nor anyone else's appearance has anything to do with their value, we haven't been able to save her from being a part of this world that values people based on what they look like. And hearing that broke my heart.

I wasn't just sad. I was angry. Angry at the patriarchy that tells little girls what they should look like and what makes them valuable. Angry at the shallowness and foolishness of our cultural values that make so many people hate themselves and superficially judge others. And you know what? I wouldn't have traded that sadness or anger for any other emotion. I wanted to feel it. And I'm glad I felt it. Because now I can act on it.

Contrary to what our cultures would often have us believe, the emotions that we often consider as "negative emotions," such as anger, sadness, and the like, are not bad things in themselves. In fact, they are quite helpful. Like any other emotion, our negative emotions are our brains telling us what's going on. If we feel happy, that's because our brain is rewarding us for doing something it wanted us to do. If we feel hurt, confused, or bitter, it's because our brain wants us to know that something isn't right.

Sometimes in spiritual circles (and especially for women), negative emotions are often seen as weak or unacceptable. It's assumed that if you get mad, it's because you're not mature enough or haven't done the spiritual work yet. And if you don't mind me saying, that's horseshit.

While it is true that the direct experience of a nondual *THIS* allows one to be free from being trapped in suffering because one is no longer attached to the desire for the world to be other than it is, that doesn't mean that enlightenment is equivalent to trading all "negative" emotions out for "positive" ones.

Freedom isn't experienced by completely avoiding emotional dissonance any more than beautiful music is made by completely avoiding anything that is not a C-major chord. In *THIS*, we may be less controlled by our circumstances and rooted in that "peace that passes all understanding," but sometimes a completely unattached joviality is not the best way to experience this world.

Imagine watching a romantic film that had a constant ticker tape running across the screen that read, "This movie is fiction . . . these characters aren't really falling in love . . . they are actors and none of this is real . . ." It would sort of ruin the vibe, right? In the same way, I've found that when I remain completely detached emotionally from the suffering around me, knowing that it is all perfect, it doesn't always help others experience their lives more fully or suffer less. Sometimes, other people suffer less when we are willing to "mourn with those who mourn." Maharaj-ji, an incredibly enlightened being who was known for always talking about how all of it is one, and how all of it is perfect, also said, "I love suffering because it brings me so close to God."

God is not distanced from the pain of humanity, sitting on a throne somewhere or waxing his beard. God is on death row. God is an addict. God is jealous that her husband spends all of his free time with his friends rather than her. And when you love God, truly and deeply love God, sometimes it's better to sit down in the mud with him and cry than to sing hymns to him about his glory.

This world is full of so much shame, fear, hate, and violence, and to embrace that level of suffering within one's experience, not simply as an unattached observer, but as a freely embodied desire, can be incredibly painful. Still, if that is how I (the All) become more free, what else could I do? An isolated detachment from desire is enough to save this particular organism from a life of suffering, but in that detachment, as I figure out who I really am (*THIS*), love is the only natural response. Love throws me back into the fray where God becomes ever so close. Here, I am free to rejoice with those who rejoice and mourn with those who mourn. Here I am free to suffer as much or as little as I desire.

This is something I'm still learning about. As an introvert, I've been happy enough in the past to stay out of the fray of relational drama, usually simply preferring a window seat in the spaceship and maybe a bucket of popcorn. Recently, however, I've been making an effort to be more emotionally present and vulnerable with those I love. So far, I have to say, it's not going all that well. For example, in a recent attempt toward connection and emotional vulnerability, I confided some things to some friends that I wouldn't normally have said for fear of being misunderstood. I hoped it would bring understanding and connection. Instead, it brought misunderstanding and hurt.

In my attempt to minimize suffering, I actually just created more suffering. So what to do?

It's almost enough to make one wonder why Buddha ever bothered getting up from the bliss he found under that Bodhi tree. Why would one bother going back into the noise and suffering of human interaction and relationship if one didn't have to? Why experience the foulness of sitting in the mud with the broken when the entire Kingdom of Heaven is yours? Why step back into the realm of maya (illusion) when one realizes one is God? Well, because, *THIS* is love. If I truly surrender to *THIS*, how can I help but be formed into the very image and embodiment of her love? The process may often be messy, reckless, and painful, but I've tasted enough of it to know that the true love of *THIS* is worth every bit of pain that it costs.

So, yeah, I'm still learning about that. How can I, a man of privilege, spout off ideas about freedom to those who don't have the luxuries, opportunities, and good health that I do? How can I embody love in a way that shares in the stories and suffering of others while at the same time embodying the peace that transcends those stories? I don't know yet. But I think it's worth the effort. And honestly, that's why I've written this book. Because the more I've seen of *THIS*, the more my heart has been opened to how your freedom is tied to mine. Like I said at the beginning, this book has been my attempt at a love letter to you to remind you of who you really are.

Our world is full of so much suffering. I feel it so acutely every time I open up my news or social media feeds. I feel it in the interactions among my family and friends and in the eyes of strangers on the street. It hurts so much.

"Momma, am I pretty?"

I feel the tension between the right and the left, the young and the old, the religious and the nonreligious. All the groups hating one another. The arguments all sound so complicated. Under it all:

"Momma, am I pretty?"

Yes, my love. You are beautiful.

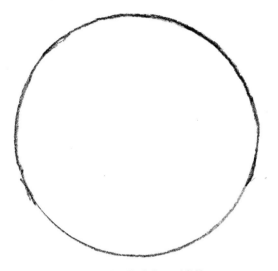

8. Forgetting Both Ox and Self

Fairy Gardens

"Do you think we are going to transform the world by lifting all the pebbles off the walks and putting precious jewels down?"
—RAM DASS

S ix thirty A.M. I'm stretched out with my two little girls on our oversized sofa that is too large for our living room. Amelie cuddles me on my left side, Lucie climbs up and snuggles across my chest. Two tiny human beings that are the very incarnation of my heart and soul. The Divine image crafted into skin, smiles, muscles, and little girls' hair. And in the case of the little one, some unknown gloob pasted across her chubby cheek. I don't even care. The moment is perfect.

I think of all we had to experience to make it to this moment. Heart surgeries. Spa floors. Betrayals and disappointments. Broken hearts and blissful sex. Ketchup-loving pastors and megachurch coffee shops. White couches and embarrassing journal entries. Purity rings and shamanic ceremonies involving magic mushrooms. How marvelous can one life be? I love it all. I love Lisa, whose body knit together these magical little souls lying on my chest. Lisa, who stayed with me, who fought and loved me fiercely through it all. I love my dad, who always loved me, and who, even after the worst failure of his life, had the courage to not only come back but to keep growing and evolving. For years, my suffering had blinded me to the generosity, strength, wisdom, and character that he so clearly exhibits and embodies, but now I am grateful to more clearly see what a remarkable man he was and is. I love my mom, who has always given so much of herself for all of us, who in the most painful time of her life somehow had the courage and grace to forgive, to love, and keep our family together. I love my siblings and friends who have been such exceptional companions through all the madness. I love my Christian upbringing. I love Bloom church and all of the deep work and great stories that it gifted us. I even love my old best friend who tried to kick us out of our own church—at least the guy had some convictions and tried to stay faithful to them. I love the churches, colleges, and festivals who also had the integrity to follow their convictions when they canceled gigs on us. I love the nurses and their machines that kept Lucie alive in the hospital. I love my heart for feeling all of this love. I love my body for carrying me through the magical illusion of space-time, allowing me to experience all of the joy, sadness, bliss, and suffering that has made this life so visceral, adventurous, and heartbreakingly beautiful.

I know that none of this will last. My girls will grow up and be too big to jump onto my chest and snuggle in the mornings in the way that they are right now.

I won't always have the good health that I enjoy now, and the remnants of my youth will continue to drain away into lines, wrinkles, torpor, and decay. Everyone and everything I know will pass into the night sky like the mist of a single breath. And that's part of the beauty of it. All of the infinite glory of the All is within this very moment, waiting to be tasted and seen.

I had lunch yesterday with a friend who is going through a divorce. He told me that it feels like the last eleven years were a waste that have emptied down the drain. I asked him why he thought that. Why would the end of a marriage mean that all of those years of his marriage had been a waste? Was there some end point in his mind's story of marriage where everything would culminate into a single moment of success? Would there be some sort of award or freeze-frame moment that suddenly made it all worth it? He laughed and admitted that he didn't know.

What exactly do we expect from the toil of our lives, jobs, and relationships? For the credits to roll as we are hoisted onto the shoulders of the cheering crowd? For the frame to eternally freeze as the girl leans in for the long kiss in the rain? Our books and movies tell us stories of varieties of happy endings, but these are never the real ending of any story. They don't show us Sleeping Beauty and Prince Charming growing old and wrangling with degenerating bodies, dreams, and relationships. They don't show how the leading man in the rom-com ends up dying of prostate cancer at sixty-eight and how his beloved wife spends the next thirty years lonely and sad until she dies from her third stroke. They never show how the football player who gets hoisted onto everybody's shoulder eventually has a slow decline in his career until he throws out his shoulder and can't play anymore. They don't show him struggling with his crippling depression and sense of meaninglessness after he retires and nobody cares.

Life isn't a prelude to a perfect freeze-frame. A life fully lived in every moment is not some foreign concept about some other reality—it is simply *THIS*. You reading this book. Scratching your ass. Feeling a little tired, cranky, or horny. *THIS* is the All in All. *THIS* is Heaven. *THIS* is the freedom you have been looking for. It is not in the specifics of the myths that we make sense of the world with. It is not with the stories you tell yourself and others about who you should be or could be. It is just *THIS*.

I asked my friend going through the divorce to remember what it was like during the "good times" of his marriage. How did those moments feel? What was he doing in the "good moments"? Taking a breath perhaps? Laughing? Sitting in a chair and talking to someone? Chewing some food? Were those married moments really all that different from these divorce moments?

It's our clinging to these stories and all of the "shoulds" and "coulds" that come with it that cause us so much suffering. We avert our gaze and our love from *THIS*, thinking that it should be or should have been *that*. We are imprisoned within these stories that minimize or even reject the present moment and instead pay attention to some illusory past or future narrative. We don't love *THIS*. We want *that*.

I am just going to school now so that I can get a job someday and finally get to my real life.

I'm just working this job for now, so I can save up money and do what I really want to do.

I'm just working so hard in my career right now so that I can buy a house.

I'm just working on paying off this house right now so I can retire and not worry about money anymore.

And then it becomes, *I just miss the good old days when . . .*

Beloved, I hate to break it to you, but the magic freeze-frame you've been wanting is never going to come. You're in the perfect moment already. If this moment is always some sort of stepping-stone in your mind to some other ideal potential moment when you finally are happy and fulfilled, you'll never be happy or fulfilled.

> Wherever your eyes and arms and heart can move
> against the earth and sky,
> the Beloved has bowed there—
> Our Beloved has bowed there
> knowing you were coming.[48]

If we were to suddenly find ourselves in Heaven in our present state of clinging to desire, what makes us think that we wouldn't suffer every bit as much as we do now? If we aren't home in the present moment, why would we be home there? Heaven is right here and right now. The meaning of life is not an abstract set of thoughts or words—it's simply and fully *THIS*. It's the cold leather of

48. Hafiz, "This Place Where You Are Now," in *The Gift: Poems by Hafiz, the Great Sufi Master*, trans. Daniel Ladinsky (New York: Penguin, 1999).

morning couches and the slight floral scent of little girls' hair. It's sunbeams pouring through the glass of the living room windows and kissing our skin with yet another new day. It's the coolness of our breath entering our nostrils and the warmth of it escaping from our lips. It's the feeling of cool, damp grass under our bare feet and the shiver up our spines after a much-needed pee.

As I lie on the couch, my heart feels wide open, and there is nothing to do or change about anything. All there is to do is experience it. No need to try to make meaning-making myths fit together or to exclude or fear any of it. All of it belongs. Here, I can love this moment and all the moments connected to it because none of this comes without all of this. The love. The suffering. The play. The adventure.

I look out the window and see a small patch of grass. I could be disappointed that it's not a bigger patch or dread that it needs to be mowed. I could also experience the wonder, remembering that from a certain vantage point, every one of those blades of grass is a universe unto itself with atomic structures like galaxies swirling and dancing through empty, God-drenched space. I could see it as a thou—the Godhead incarnating not only as the grass itself but as the fruit of an ecosystem of unseen life, energy, and mystery. I could even experience it as my very Self—every single blade of grass, reflecting photon, and swirl of emptiness within emptiness a part of my own body that is the All. In this perspective, the grass becomes part of my own skin. The morning sky becomes a bright expanse of my own consciousness. The birds chirping are the songs in my head, and the breeze is the great Spirit, my very breath. Or I could not think anything at all, and just be—letting all my mythical constructs fade from my mind and directly experience pure nondual, empty awareness where there is only *THIS*.

There is a famous story that is told about the origin of Zen Buddhism in which the Buddha, Siddhārtha Gautama, presents a wordless sermon by simply holding up a white flower before his disciples. The only one to understand the sermon was the disciple Mahākāśyapa, who is said to have smiled in response.

The secret at the heart of that and every flower is the direct wisdom of suchness—it is the experience of *THIS*.

To realize the beholder is the beheld is the secret at the heart of every rose.

The entire universe is being presented at every moment as the Buddha's wordless sermon. Every flower, blade of grass, sunbeam, heartbeat, and period at the end of a sentence is Incarnation—Word becoming flesh, void becoming form. Our direct awareness of it all is the Goddess gazing at and as herself, fully and wildly naked and *THIS*. He is the crucified one, broken and poured out for the good and possibility of the world. She is the wounded one who eats of the fruit of knowledge in order to give birth to herself, even if that means temporarily lying to herself in the form of serpents and other forms of embodied patriarchy like popes, priests, and presidents. It is in the full and direct experience of *THIS* that Wisdom rings out:

> In this moment, Behold thyself, resplendent Queen who is everything and everyone. Thou art seen. Thou art known. Thou art loved.

I love the mixture of all these myths and metaphors that have formed my experience of this magnificent existence. Holding them loosely, I feel like a child again. Unencumbered. Free to play, to sing, to dance before I knew what "good" playing, singing, or dancing was supposed to look like.

My daughter Amelie has a fairy garden in our backyard. I don't know exactly where it is or what marvels it holds. She doesn't feel the need to show me that, and that's okay with me. I know it's a secret place for her that is magical and special and as real as anything else because it's part of her imagination and therefore her experience.

The way I see it now, all of our myths and worldviews, all of our religions and political structures, every language and book and empire—they're all our fairy gardens, constructs of imagination that allow us to have the experiences that are to happen in this particular game of God-made-flesh. If we don't hold on too fiercely, we'll grow up eventually and the gardens will evolve. Maybe someday I'll see that all of my running about from tree to tree is immature and will find the need to constrict my usage of metaphors. But now I feel young, alive, and free. I am like a young seedling who fell from the branches of these great and wise elders. Much of the time, I run around with various twigs from different trees in my hand—Vishnu Dass, lover of Christ, student of the Buddha. Perhaps I too often do not give the ancient stories the respect they deserve—thinking that I can casually dismiss entire branches of these giants with a chuckle and a turn of the head, and mindlessly opt instead for the flexibility and logging potential of the younger and less-established trees. But I am still learning. I am still listening. And as all those commercials for the United Church of Christ say, "God is still speaking."

So what kind of games will God play with this life I'm experiencing? I would enjoy spending my life playing in a way that results in less suffering for people who are really deeply trapped within it. I'd love to spend my imagination on delightful games like making music, writing books, and having silly dance parties with my girls rather than on other games like boredom, war, or hatred. I'd love to play like a child who loses himself in his play, but not to the point where I lose the knowledge that it is a game. I'd love to live the kind of life that Guru Jesus taught us about—a life to the fullest. A life with more love than fear. More faith than cynicism. Jesus knew that the full reality of *THIS* was beyond words, so rather than formulating doctrines or dogmas made of words that most of us forget are inherently made of stories, he usually told the stories more directly.

And that's why, in writing this book, I didn't want to just give you words and ideas. I wanted to also share with you some of my story, because that's where I've experienced *THIS*. And as such, it is your story, too. The words, ideas, and fairy gardens are lovely enough, but they are abstractions, not the *truth* itself. All of the words in this book are just more myths to play with and then let go of. I'm no guru for you to follow. I'm just God playing the part of a flighty, absurdist musician living in Los Angeles. I have no life-changing wisdom to offer you that hasn't been written a thousand times before, but I, too, have looked at the flowers and seen that there is nothing to worry about. I, like you, too, perhaps, beloved, have felt deep betrayal, crippling depression, and tremendous pain, and yet here I am, still alive and with magical twenty-one-chromosomed baby gloob on my chest, and I wouldn't have it any other way. How could I? Have you heard this Music? It's everything.

9. Reaching the Source

Acknowledgments

Lisa, Guzlam, Isla, my soul, my heart, thank you for sharing your life with me and teaching me so much about *THIS*.

Amelie, my fairy princess. You make my life magical, and I love you more than words can say.

Lu, you are God's very kiss on my cheek. Never stop being a rascal.

Mom and dad. I am so proud to be your son. Part of me hopes that you don't read this book, as there are parts of it that you probably will not enjoy reading very much, but I want you and everyone else to know how happy I am to have parents like you. This book contains a lot of my old drama, but there was so much more good than bad in my life, and I will always be grateful to both of you for all the love and life that you gave me.

Mike McHargue, my business partner and dearest friend, you are a strange and wonderful creature, and you make my life so rich. Your thoughts and perspectives have always sharpened and challenged me, and this book is definitely better for it.

Robert, David, Lissa, what a joy to be your big brother. You all make me proud. Don't tell mom about the mushrooms part in the book.

Nancy, your editing was a lifesaver for this book. To work with someone who "sees" was very important for me, and I am so happy to have come across your path. Thank you for all the hard work and inspiring conversation.

To Chris, Jan, and everybody else at Roundtree, thank you for partnering with me on this endeavor. Not many publishing companies would extend the trust and freedom that I felt working with you. Thank you for believing in me and in this book. I'm honored to be able to share it with the world with you.

To all my friends and family and listeners and readers and meditators: thank you for making my life the most magnificent journey I could imagine. This book is for you.

Library of Congress Cataloging-in-Publication Data available.

ISBN: 978-1-944903-61-9

10 9 8 7 6 5 4 3 2 1

Manufactured in China

Publisher: Chris Gruener
Creative Director: Iain Morris
Designer: Rob Dolgaard
Managing Editor: Jan Hughes
Editorial Assistant: Mason Harper

 Roundtree Press
149 Kentucky Street, Suite 7
Petaluma, CA 94952
www.roundtreepress.com

10. Returning to the World